The Best of Border Voices

Poet Laureates, Pulitzer-Prize Winners & the Wisdom of Kids

By Jack Webb,
Founder-Director, Border Voices Poetry Project

Level 4 Press, Inc.

Editor: Jack Webb
Assistant Editor: Chris Dickerson

Introduction & biographies of poets: Jack Webb

This book is printed on acid-free paper.

Published by
Level 4 Press, Inc.
13518 Jamul Drive
Jamul, CA 91935
www.level4press.com

BISAC Subject Heading: POE001000 POETRY / Anthologies (multiple authors)
Library of Congress Control Number: 2006937617

ISBN: 978-193376924-0

Printed in China

Dedication

This book, like many of the
poems in it, is
"woven out of love's loose ends;
for myself and for my friends." *

---

* With a grateful nod to Oxford poet Jon Stallworthy, from
whom this phrase is borrowed. Stallworthy had been criti-
cized for not writing anti-war or anti-capitalist poems. He
indicated, with this phrase, that his poems had a higher,
or at least a different, purpose than purely political re-
form.

Table of Contents

Preface

That Happy Plunge into Uncertainty

By Jack Webb
Founder-Director, Border Voices Poetry Project

> *"Education is an admirable thing, but it is well to remember from time to time that nothing that is worth knowing can be taught."* **— Oscar Wilde**

Like most writers, I seem to have the most success when I plunge directly into the heart of my uncertainty. And right now that uncertainty comes in the form of a swirl of images and sounds:

. . . **the shy face** of a Mexican-American boy, never looking up as he stands onstage before a crowd of 1,000 people, reading a poem (it seemed at the time) to an invisible ant crawling across his shoe. How his parents beamed, how the TV cameras whirred, the people cheering ...

. . . **Maya Angelou chanting** her poems to 7,500 people at San Diego's Cox Arena; a 9-year-old black girl on the same stage, reciting Maya's most famous poem: "Still I Rise . . . " The girl's huge brown eyes filling the movie screen hanging above the darkened stage, the camera swinging in for a spotlighted close-up. "I rise . . . " She lengthens that last syllable, draws it out into a sigh, into a sonic banner above the awed arena . . .

. . . **Lawrence Ferlinghetti's bald head turning red** as a teen-ager plants a kiss in the middle of his forehead. "I didn't think 78-year-old poets had groupies!" says one stunned and admiring worker at the 1997 Border Voices Poetry Fair . . .

. . . **the weird beeping** five minutes ago, as an e-mail caromed out of the Internet and deposited itself in my computer. It was a message from Billy Collins, the former U.S. poet laureate with the winsome smile and irrepressible humor. Yes, says Billy: he WILL contribute one of his poems to the book that you, the reader, now hold in your hand.

Images, sounds ... night sweats and daytime jitters ... the rogue memories of 14 years proliferating like mutant weeds in my sleep-deprived brain as I labor on this introduction. Thus the uncertainty: where to start? And out of uncertainty, a bit of creativity: Seek the essential. What does THIS book offer you, the reader? WHY is it worth your while to buy it? Even better, just how much FUN will it be for you to read it?

Well, it WILL be fun. In this book you'll find some of the greatest and most entertaining writers in the world today, with little whimsical anecdotes about what they're REALLY like behind-the-scenes at poetry fairs. 60 great writers came to San Diego for Border Voices Poetry Fairs, and male and female, young and old, they were ALL a lot of fun: they impressed kids, educated parents, knew how to party, and in general turned San Diego into a literary Mecca (or at least a literary halfway house) starting in 1994.

A good chunk of those 60 poets contributed poems to this book. Some of their poems are published here for the first time; other poems were featured at the various poetry fairs where they read, or in the annual Border Voices anthologies.

You'll also find poems by some of the thousands of kids who've taken Border Voices poetry workshops and appeared on Border Voices TV shows, or in those annual anthologies, since 1994. THOSE poems may be the best part of the book. As Billy Collins said, back in 2002: "I'm jealous of their energy."

You'll also meet the Border Voices poet-teachers, the men and women who go into the schools to teach students how to find their voices. Parents will find this section of SPECIAL interest: these are the poets whose talents have reinvigorated classrooms. Teachers have reported significant increases in scores on standardized tests following Border Voices workshops: for example, some students achieved an astonishing **200-point jump** on the verbal portion of the Scholastic Aptitude Test — enough to enable a student who might have been heading towards a career as a hamburger flipper to qualify for a scholarship to Harvard. These teacher testimonials were confirmed by a recent study, financed by the California Arts Council, that showed Border Voices poetry workshops at San Diego's Pershing Middle School producing "huge and continuing increases in scores on standardized English tests."

*   *   *

"Art is the most intense mode of individualism that the world has known."   — **Oscar Wilde**

Looked at one way, Border Voices is a nonprofit organization under the umbrella of the SDSU Research Foundation, the "fiscal receiver" for the project.

Looked at another way, Border Voices is as tenuous as a cloud, a vortex of hopes and dreams based on a very simple idea ...

I'll bet you noticed the Oscar Wilde quote that leads off this section. You may even have wondered why there are TWO Wilde quotes in this introduction. What's all this about Oscar Wilde, anyway?

Well, Oscar Wilde was an absolutely opinionated and witty individual, a man who'd found

xvi

his own voice. And that's what Border Voices tries to help kids do, and (if the schools are right) has done very successfully: it gives kids a way to find their own voices, and encourages and honors the resulting boost in individuality as well as test scores (that academic boost is, from my point of view, nice ... but secondary to the life-potentiating effect of actually FINDING one's own Self).

To put it another way: what the kids have found through poetry is what many people (including myself) have discovered by using this amazing tool. All of us — you know this is true — secretly hope that we will someday find that one very SPECIAL person: the mentor, the master, the person of sensitivity, some keen intellect possessing sufficient wisdom and insight to look at our life, spread it out like a great illuminated plain below us, and VALIDATE it, telling us that what we have done is GOOD.

As we all learn if we are lucky, that special person is our own Self, illuminated by art, and with our quixotic mistakes justified, somehow, after all.

*   *   *

Now you can, if you wish, go on to the main part of the book. If, instead, you're interested in learning more about how Border Voices works, we can do that in the next two sections of this introduction, using the poetic techniques of "juxtaposition" and "association" rather than pure logic.

The first step in our creative experiment will be a Border Voices lesson plan, previously published, that is used to help kids bring the marvelous into their writing. It is a tool to unlock the imagination, one of many used by Border Voices poets in classrooms throughout San Diego. As you read it, and perhaps experiment with its suggested approach to writing, you will begin to see how the young poets printed elsewhere in this book were able to craft works of great beauty.

Immediately after the lesson plan, you will find selected excerpts from a creative diary I kept during many hours spent recuperating from four heart operations over the past year. The diary helped me understand what I was trying to do as a poet, and as the founder of Border Voices.

A QUICK NOTE BEFORE WE BEGIN: you may also enjoy reading the biographies of our featured poets. They have been updated since they first appeared in the anthologies printed annually from 1994 through 2006. However, the underlying playfulness remains unchanged. In addition, it may be of special interest to teachers and others that the FORMAT of the biographies has differed from year to year. That's because the goals for the anthology introductions changed slightly over time. At one point, the aim was to provide kids with more information about the rough-and-tumble world of the professional writer; sometimes the emphasis was on technique. The result of this diversity is that the biographies as a WHOLE present a rich tapestry of approaches to modern poetry.

Step 1 in the Experiment:
A Lesson Plan on Magic and Poetry

> *"You see there are in our countries rivers which have no names, trees which nobody knows, and birds which nobody has described . . . Our duty, then, as we understand it, is to express what is unheard of."* — **Pablo Neruda**

There are many different ways of approaching poetry, but they all have one thing in common — they are methods by which the poet can "kick-start" his or her imagination, forcing it to break out of conventional or learned ways of thinking and writing. One such technique is "magic realism," in which the poet introduces myths, ghosts and dreams into the reality of his life. Also called *lo real marvilloso*, or the marvelous real, this technique is especially appealing to younger students, but also exciting for older students as well as adults.

At the beginning of the class, the Border Voices poet gives the students a few examples of poems that have an element of magic. The poet may also talk about how the human voice is the greatest of all musical instruments, and that if they learn to use it well, it will serve them well. If they wish to be lawyers, they will be more persuasive lawyers if they become adept at "playing" the rhythms of their voices. If they wish to be writers . . . or dancers . . . or actresses . . . they also have something to learn from this class.

The next step is for the poet to help students write their own magical realism poem. The poet proceeds as follows, pausing after each step to give the students a chance to write:

(1) Think of something you really want, something that is difficult or perhaps even impossible to achieve. Maybe you want to get an "A" on that oh-so-difficult history or math test, or perhaps someone close to you is ill and you would like to see them get well quickly. Maybe there is a pet you'd really like, a thoroughbred horse or a rare Tibetan dog, that you or your parents can't afford. Take a minute or two and write what you would like to have, preferably in one sentence.

(2) In one sentence, give a physical description of yourself. Are you bald? (LAUGHTER) Do you wear jewelry? Is your skin tanned or light, do you wear tattoos like Dennis Rodman? (MORE LAUGHTER) Be as accurate and vivid as possible.

(3) If the poem is about someone else, and what you would like for them, then write a physical description of the beneficiary of your magic-wish poem. Do they have eyes like walnuts, hair curved like a seashell? Find two or three things about them that are really "them," so that we would recognize them if we saw them in a crowd. "Oh yes, there's the tattooed lady with the seashell hair."

(4) Now imagine yourself (or the subject of the poem) trying to do the impossible thing, and failing. Describe what that's like, again in one or two sentences.

(5) Now imagine something magical that would let you achieve the thing you want. Perhaps it's an elixir that will turn you into a genius for a day, so you can write that history paper in a way that will wow your teacher. Perhaps it's a mysterious billfold you find on the street, with one dollar in it; but when you pull the dollar out, another dollar magically appears in its place, and this continues until you have a huge pile of bills at your feet. In one or two sentences, describe the magical object, what it looks like, what it does.

(6) Again, in one or two sentences, describe what happens when you use the magical object to achieve your desires. You get exactly what you want — how does it make you feel? Are you happy? A little disappointed? Are there unexpected side-effects (your seashell hair turns blue, for example)?

(7) Now write down all those sentences as one poem. Feel free to juggle the words and lines around. When you're done, hand the poem to a classmate and let him look it over and make suggestions. You, of course, will be doing the same with his or her poem. Use any of the suggestions that feel "right" to you.

Step 2 in the Experiment: Excerpts from A Creative Diary, 2005-06

10/12/05 — Much of the psychiatric literature about relationships treats most interpersonal experience as disease syndromes. Better if we treat such relationships, and their various permutations, as creative acts, and bring the tools of creativity to them. Then we will see that beginners are usually a bit inept — though not diseased — and tend to copy the patterns of others, as Bob Dylan imitated Muddy Waters, muddying his own creative waters until he found his own voice (a hammering together of various sounds and rhythms in a new way) and sang out clearly, saying: "and the chains of the sea will have busted in the night, and be buried on the bottom of the ocean."

10.13.05 — I was thinking about myth-making and that brilliant myth-making quack, Dr. Freud. All these general theories of existence (paganism, Islam, Buddhism, psychoanalysis, etc.) are marked by two things which tend to persuade: internal consistency, and something external they can point to which seems to fit within the proposed paradigm. With Islam, we have the "miracle" of the Koran and various assorted mini-miracles, such as the prophet feeding 1,000 men (more or less) with a single sheep. Psychoanalysis points to things (troubles between daughters and fathers, mothers and sons) and invents the Oedipus and Electra complexes to explain things which I think are mainly failures of creativity.

Paganism could point at things which were MUCH more convincing. They actually SAW Jove's spears flying across the sky, the great *astrapln,* bolts of lightning, sharp as a demon's horns. The Greeks were not fools. They knew mystery when they saw it.

11.12.05 — XXX sent me some prose-poems he'd been working on and added:

> I hope you like what I've sent, but sometimes when I think of the world, these little artistic and philanthropic spasms of ours seem so futile and self-serving. It's hard to be putting so much of a life and effort into something so fragile.

I replied:

Demons may be more powerful, but that doesn't make the flower or the lamb irrelevant.

11/15/05 — Went to the SDSU Foundation today, and found that Than, the secretary, had taken roses from the bouquet I gave her office and dried them.

It suggested to me — as I told her and Chrissy (the grant administrator)– a possible reply to the poem written by the Japanese poet Issa, after the death of his daughter:

> The world of dew
> Is the world of dew
> And yet, and yet . . .

In a short commentary on this poem, Issa wrote that ". . . I knew well it was no use to cry, that water once flown past the bridge does not return, and blossoms that are scattered are beyond recall. Yet try as I would, I could not, simply could not, cut the binding cord of human love."

But Issa!!! Roses do not have to be beyond recall! Than, through creativity, has preserved her roses. You, through your poem and commentary, have preserved your love for your daughter.

This is what we offer each other, this little thing — not real gods, but the gods we create out of our love and compassion, our science and our poetry.

12/11/05 — Cavemen created their mythos of Bear gods and Lion gods as they shivered around their campfires in the dark of night. The Persian Zoroaster was the first to improve on this concept, suggesting that a single god ("Ahura Mazda") ruled and created the world. With the invention of novels, movies, and the Internet, the number of mythos have expanded exponentially, and as a result people are beginning to suspect that mythos are interchangeable.

What may be more difficult to realize is that personalities are mythos too. A dominant one today among white Westerners is the one invented by Hemingway — the craftsman hero of "The Old Man and The Sea" as well as "The Sun Also Rises" and Hemingway himself in "A Moveable Feast" — making sense out of himself and the world by attention to craft. We see that hero again and again, and its presence convinces us we are in the presence of great art.

This is easy, too easy. There are other great personas, a little more difficult of imitation either artistically or personally: Sir Isaac Newton; the multisyllabic and chameleon-like Finley Wren in the book of the same name (by Phillip Wylie), and so on.

Recognition of THIS possibility opens another possibility—that every day is a new day, open to inhabitation by another persona from our chameleon-like natures. It also throws into disarray all established world and other-world systems and psychologies, including Freudianism with its clockwork psychological mechanisms (Oedipus complex, etc.), which attempts to portray human beings as wind-up toys with an occasional spring loose, just waiting for the analytical screwdriver . . .

12.20.05 — If we step OUT of the myths, we can have a good and entertaining time, and maybe help each other.

1/15/05 — More and more, humanity seems to me, in the mass, to be a great unconscious animal, turning and trembling as it dreams. We can hope to teach it sweeter dreams.

2/18/06 — It's raining, which seems the perfect punctuation mark for a night of dreams and reverie — underlining, as it does, that nature WILL have its way, no matter how we pave the world with asphalt, no matter what abstractions we weave around our affairs.

2.25.06 — KAFKA QUOTE: "You do not even have to leave your room. Remain sitting at your table and listen. Do not even listen, simply wait. Do not even wait, remain still and solitary. The world will freely offer itself to you unasked. It has no choice. It will roll in ecstasy at your feet."

9/24/06 — A lovely quote from Thomas Merton, the Trappist monk, found in the Fall newsletter from the California Council for the Humanities:

> "The rush and pressure of modern life are a form, perhaps the most common form, of its innate violence. To allow oneself to be carried away by a multitude of conflicting concerns, to surrender to too many demands, to commit oneself to too many projects. To want to help everyone in everything is to succumb to violence."

That's me, all right, at least as I've been most of the last 40 years. I seem to be pulling back from it now . . . although even my meditations, begun in desperation, have somehow developed a secondary goal that seems to be growing in importance in the back of my mind: to help others (everyone?) by editing and publishing them . . . showing them how to do it, from the very beginning of the creative act . . .

I will ponder this. Perhaps I will keep the meditations to myself, at least til I have examined this little puzzle more fully . . . I don't want to abort a process that is proving so personally beneficial, by turning it into a public act . . . or even worse, a COMMERCIAL act . . .

. . . although MAYBE . . . just . . . maybe . . . I could write a BOOK, full of funny and endearing stories about the great writers we've brought to San Diego, a book filled with poetry . . . with an introduction that would hint, in the gentlest possible way, about where to find the creative impulse amid all the regimented dreck, drama and dreariness of modern life . . . I could title this essay so that the title ITSELF is a key to the mystery, perhaps something like . . . YES!!! . . . "That Happy Plunge into Uncertainty" . . .

PREFACE

Student Poems

"Who can move best but the inspired child of his times?" — **Eudora Welty**

On Dec. 10, 2002 — two months before he became the ninth chairman of the National Endowment for the Arts — Dana Gioia made a lightning visit to San Diego to appear on a TV show with some Border Voices students. Gioia had already achieved worldwide fame as a poet and literary critic. His televised remarks, transcribed below, provide a cogent and inspiring introduction to the student poems on the next few pages.

DANA GIOIA: There's something magical about the poems that children write, if we let them. Adults look at a fire hydrant, and see a fire hydrant. A child sees a castle, or a robot, or a rocket ship . . . a child has a brilliance with words, a discovered love of language, and the ability to play with those words, turning them into charmingly unexpected visions . . .

Like many writers and educators, I have a dream of bringing major poets into the schools . . . and promoting poetry in every classroom. That vision has already begun in San Diego, thanks to the Border Voices Poetry Project . . .

[In the next few pages you can] experience how poetry becomes remarkable, when it is informed by the rhythm of a child's voice and imagination . . .

Grade One

Smoke
By Amanda Barnard

My dad with his brown hair
is in his room.
He is touching a cigarette,
and he is smoking.
I am watching him.
I am watching him from my room.

If I Was Homework
By Gavin Carpenter

If I was homework,
I would burn for you
and crumple for you and tear
and jump in the fire for you.

The Grain of Water
By Justin Tafel

The water is like a choir.
It sings so pretty
I listen and
feel the beat
soft as wood grain.

Grade Two

Guitar Remembers
By Nicole Drago

The guitar remembers being a tree, and
the guitar remembers hearing the birds tweet
    and
the flowers bowing in the wind.
I want you to reach up and tell how the guitar
missed being a tree and
How the guitar missed hearing the birds
and the flowers in the wind.
Don't look at the sky.
Don't look at the grass.
Hear the guitar and how it misses being a tree.

Uncle Mark's Telescope
By Marie Gonzales

When I looked in the telescope,
in the twinkling sky,
it reminded me of my Uncle Mark.
I miss my Uncle Mark.
He is dead.
We miss him.
I drew him with a marker.
He died because of cancer.
He was smoking, that is how he's dead.
It was a good memory in that twinkling sky.
I think he can hear me say these words,
twinkling telescope,
moon man,
memory telescope.

Behind My Eyes
By Karli Kroeker

My hands are vines reaching for the top of the
wall.
In my chest sits the candle of life lighting up
my body.
My legs are trees trying to grow to the sky.
Between my fingers swirls the breath of every
creature on earth.
Behind my eyes sit the pictures of dreams.
Under my feet flowers grow and tickle my toes.
Words like sweet candy sit on the tip of my
tongue.

Grade Three

Poetry Rain
By Alex Cossio

To me, poetry is an unusual rain
that makes me want to use my imagination.
It's like a double-jeopardy wheel-of-fortune.
Poetry is important because it feeds my soul
like water that soothes my heart
so it doesn't explode when I run
faster than the speed of light.
Poetry is like icicles
that freeze words on paper.

The Spider
By David Draskovich

The black spider is the dark side of the moon.
It's as hairy as your grandmother's legs.
It yells for bugs the size of kingdom come,
and his web can stop time forever.

An Old Crying Man
By Henry Fung

His sadness is like a hurricane.
His tears are like a river
running down into a canyon
being destroyed.
His eyebrows are like rain falling
from the sky.

The War, by Hannibal Sonderogger

Rainsteps
By Nicole Gilbert

My Grandma Patter passed away.
But I see
her still
sitting in her wheelchair.
It's cold and rainy outside,
but inside she's rolling
her wheelchair into the kitchen.
I can still see her,
smell her perfume,

hear her heart beating almost
like her heart is trying to get out.
She comes and gives me a kiss
as big as an ocean.
Her kiss crashes on my cheek.
You can still hear the rain drip-dropping.
Her heart beats faster and faster,
the beat of dancing.

Poetry
By Amy Inman

Poetry is like flips on the wet, soft grass.
Poetry makes me feel good.
It is music.

Poetry is magical, like the stars.
I love poetry.
It looks like indigo violet.

Poetry tastes like strawberries and all other
    kinds of fruit.
It is as sweet as an angel.
It is the best adventure ever.

Poetry is the All-Star thing.
It is like the jingle of Santa's bells.
It is the animal of life.

The Doll's House
By Vina Keophilaone

The green picture book
is square and sits
on the white table.
The book looks like a doll's house.
It shows a little girl and a little boy
on the cover
looking at the moon.
I like the book because is it like a soul
was caught in the book
a child's soul, never to escape
until someone reads the book.

Dear Mom
By Danika Lund

I'm sorry that I cut
your hair while you
were sleeping and put
lipstick all over your face.

I just wanted
you to look beautiful
like Julia Roberts.

Sadness, by Rayna Vergara

In-Your-Heart Rainbow
By Teresa Lugo

If I were a rainbow,
I would get up in the morning for you.
I would let it rain for you, so
your flowers could blossom, so
you could pick them.
I would come out when
the sun comes to see you pick flowers.
My colors are in your heart.

Ode to a Turkey
By Violet Naegele

Bob was a turkey
who lived in our backyard
in the dog house.
He was an awesome turkey.
I loved him and he loved me.

Bob was huge and had
a beautiful red beard.
His shiny green tail
was larger than his body.

I begged them not to
bake Bob but they deep fried him
in the backyard on three sticks. Dad
held his body and his friend, Larry,
held his legs, while they
poked sticks into Bob.

They put him over the same flames
where we toast marshmallows.
Dad stood on one side and Larry
on the other, as they turned
the sticks and roasted Bob
for four hours.

When Bob came to the table
I screamed and cried.
But when dad dished him up,
I tried Bob...he was delicious!
We ate all of him.

I Am Ashley
By Ashley Nauta

But when I think of my middle name,
Marie, I'm a Mexican dancer
with lots of make-up. I have a big
red, blue, yellow and green skirt on
and a top to go with it.
When I'm done performing,
I go to a taco shop to eat
but everyone wants my autograph.
I tell them not today,
but they just ignore me.
Then I'm the wind, dancing
up and around in the sky.
I like my name and don't
want to change it. I don't want
to lose that Mexican feeling.

A Suitcase Full of Chocolate
By Ryan Trumbach

I will give you an ocean
of *Sports Illustrated* books that you will love.
I will give you a year at Knotts' Berry farm
and I will be there, too.
I will give you a day of eating whatever you want
or a dream of an all-toppings pizza.
I will give you all the Zorro movies ever made
or a cave of all the riches in the world.
Let me give you a suitcase of chocolate balls
or a truck load of love.
I will give you an exploding volcano
full of basketball, baseball, and football cards.

12

I will give you a week off your job
or a dream of puppies trying to lick you.
All this I will give my dad . . .

Grade Four

My Grandma
By Joe Bridgman

My grandma Rita died
and went to heaven.
She is watching over me
like a hawk.
She likes it up there.
She is having fun
with her husband again.
She misses the people
she left that day
in the car.
The drunk took
something away
from me that
I may never see
again.
We miss her
I miss her
but I will always
love her.
She went up to heaven
in a puff
of smoke.

Hurricane Alex
By Alex Cossio

I am coming, coming to clean up
your dirty ugly mess.
I shall freeze your lips
while you shout at the top of your lungs,
"Get in the basement! Get in the basement!"
I sound like a tiger when my winds rumble.
I feel like darts hitting your face.
I smell like spring flowers, but I look like
a fierce bully on the playground at noon.
I am coming, coming to refresh the world.
Now you know that I am watching
with my great big eye.

Poetry
By Gabriel Cossio

Poetry is love and magical systems
that go around in your head.
Then you say, "I will write poetry
for the rest of my life."

Poetry to me is a brand new feather
that has fallen from a baby parrot,
bluer than the sky sparkling in my eyes.

Poetry is like the pictures in my mind,
a kaleidoscope of my grandma's crazy quilt.

The Wind Is a Wonder
By Cameron Hughes

If I were the wind
I would bring terror
Upon sailboats.
I would make it possible
For kites to fly.

When I'm mad,
I'm called a tornado.
On the rampage,
I'm called a Santa Ana.
My favorite is winter,
When I'm called a
Trade Wind.

I will come to visit.
You won't see me,
The trees will tell you.

Tortilla Magic
By Kathryn Imler

A Dalmatian tortilla
holds the family in its thin flour coat
a magic mouth-watering, heart-warming,   siz-
zling taste
Tortilla magic seizes me
It burns me with its volcanic softness
As the monstrous heap
starts molding back into a ball
I will pat it again
it will unfold

Tortilla, an unspoken memory
Tortillas consume me
until I disappear
into the magic world where they came from
A brown and white world continues to dance
Magically tortillas start sizzling
Again I wake up from my dream
the tortilla is gone
My mother calls me for dinner
She says it's tortilla night
The soft Dalmatian tortilla
holds the family together

Nasty Icky Lima Beans
By Collier Jones

Nasty icky lima beans taste
like terrible words
like on the nasty talk show Jerry Springer.
And then those very sad people jump up
and out of their chairs and
beat the living lima beans out of each other.

No Color
By Rachelle Joseph

Being invisible means no color
    clear as a diamond
    invisible as a ghost.
Having no color means being empty.
But being human means
we can never run away
from our own color.

Poetry
By Jacob Katz

Martin Luther King, Honest Abe, Rosa Parks—
people who saved the day

you think they are the nicest
people that ever were, but back then
people hated them.

They freed us all.

A Leaf
By Jasmine Lai

I am a leaf
The highest leaf on a tree.
Many are like me, others are not.
Some are green
Some are brown
Some are yellow with little holes in them.
The sun shines on me
The rain taps on me
The moon gives tender light
unlike the sun—giving hot, scorching light.
As the days pass by, I turn from small to big
from green to yellow.

One day, I fall from my home so high
to the dusty and muddy ground.
There I meet more leaves, all are brown.
I am brown too.
I am hard, not soft
I am old now, not young.

A dark day, the wind blows furiously
and all the leaves blow away
far away.
And I am with them.
I am now in a different and strange place.
No friends
no place to call home.

My Uncle, My Aunt and I
By Ana Manriquez

My uncle lies dead in his coffin
with nobody at his funeral.

I was the only one there
with my aunt.

I sat on my aunt's lap,
crying.

Grandfather Lorenzo
By Emmanuel Mercado

My grandfather is like a star
as far away as TJ.
I will always remember that cowboy hat
with a feather like a rainbow
after rain from the big blue sky
and all those funny jokes.
He teaches me that love
can not keep us apart
like borders and countries.

Couch Football
By Nicole Midstokke

My dad sits on the couch,
football on the T.V.
He eats chips,
drinks Coke,
just sitting there
watching football,
eating chips,
drinking Coke.
Then one of the teams scores!
No noise.
He just sits there.

Cactus Flower
By Bianca Miles

Beautiful hot-pink flowers,
one still closed, turning pale pink.
The fading cactus is as mean-looking as a
	villain,
the hot pink petals as glossy as lips.
Life like this doesn't go on forever.
One day, you're happy to be alive.
Then you're dead...Poof!
Just like that.

On a Clear Night
By Gina Mortensen

A beautiful fairy, with skin as smooth
as the silvery moon and a dress
as shimmery as the sun, sits

with her baby fairies, fragile as dolls
dancing about her with their tulip
dresses and rose petal aprons
waving white lanterns about them.
On this clear night
deep in the globe-green forest
the fairy queen tells me to come
watch them dance and learn their magic.

Talkative and Boasting "B"
By Alexandra Rex

Boasting B
was beautiful
and bashful as butter.
She always butted in line
and said "Bah" to beans.
Her brother
came bouncing
back from Boston.
Together they went
to Bermuda.
They found two Ts
and both of them married.
Now B was T,
tall and talkative.
Together they traveled
all over the territory
to Tennessee,
Texas and Tucson.
They ate tacos
and tamales all the time!
They traveled together
for the rest of their
tall tale lives.

Oso Temblor

By Purificación Sánchez

El está acostado
en una cama chica.

En el cuarto alumbrado,
no se le nota ni una arruga en al cara.

Por esta bien acobijado del frío,
parece un oso.

Temblando del frío,
parece que esta pasando por un temblor.

Earthquake Bear

He lies on
a small bed.

In the lighted room,
you don't notice a wrinkle on his face.

Because he is covered with blankets from the
cold,
he looks like a big bear.

Shivering from the cold,
it seems as if he is passing through an
earthquake.

Poetry in Flight
By Geoffrey Scholl

Poetry is
whales breaching, flying
fish over a waterfall.
Poetry is written
words stuck
in a dictionary
that I open.
Boom!
The words fly out.

I See
By Mitchell Seaman

I see orange and purple flowers
of fluffy clouds as white as a sheep's wool
and wonder,
Where do you
go
when you die?

You go up on top
of one
of
those
clouds

that sing down to Earth.
Some people would
die to hear that music,

so they do.

Peacock's Dream
By Jordan Sewell

Peacock dreams of a duller world
a world of only black and white.
He dreams of no hunters or poachers
he dreams that he is ordinary.

For all his colors
and feathered crown
bore him to sleep
to dream this dream.

I Used to . . . But Now
By Alex Stromberger

I used to walk through a magical
doorway inside a rainbow of roses,
daisies, violets, marigolds, and
    chrysanthemums.
I could see mountains of
music, trees of moonlight, animals
of stars, and flowers of sunlight.
I would jump so high I could reach
the silver moonbirds that never
stop flying and play with the
stars. It was beautiful then, when
daytime shone upon the earth,
but now it is night, night,
night.

Road Voice

By Jessica Swenson

On a lonely road at night
I heard something calling me.
I looked to one side
    then the other.
I looked in front
    I looked in back.
And in back of me
there was a wolf.
The voice was nice sounding.
It said, "I am homeless.
I want some food.
Please let me stay for the night."
I said back, "I am lost.
    I don't know where I am
    or where my home is."
The wolf said, "Well, on this road
you will never find your home.
This road goes around in circles.
Believe me,
I have tried."

The Brown Leaf

By Claire Tompkins

The brown leaf on the road
remembers the big oak tree.
The white snow drifts
getting larger. The
red, green, yellow, orange, and other
brown leaves, slowly drifting down.

I want you to see the
leaf, not a bright cheerful leaf,
but the brown leaf slowly
moving with the others
in the wind.

When you pick up the brown leaf,
take it home,
trace it,
make it more beautiful.

Abel
By Nefi Varela

Abel,
I am so sorry that
I pushed you in the mud.

You looked like a
wet dog splashing,
like a pig rolling in his pen.

I really enjoyed watching you squiggle.

My Heart
By Jerardo Velez

My heart is big like poetry.
My heart likes red and green
and goes, ptt, ptt, ptt, ptt.

Sometimes, it says "help."

26

Grade Five

My Family
By David Bishop

I take a glance
at the pictures of
my real parents.
I'll never know why
they gave me away,
and before I even
got to know them.

Now all I have of
them is a couple
treasured pictures and
a letter every year.
I don't think
that's enough.
All I want is a little more letters
and some more pictures.

But then three years
later my parents that
adopted me broke up,
just as the chain links
were connecting and I
was getting used to
my new home. Now,
I'm as sad as a crow.

Dances of the Dead
By Erin Byrne

Sweet *pan de muerte* sits
On the beautiful altars' tops.
Bright decorations border lonely Mexico
While the sugar happy skulls dance.
People remember a short breath
Is one step closer to death.
Sugar skulls sing to the bright stars
While marigold petals dance on the cold
    ground.
Delicious food welcomes lost spirits
To the houses of their loved ones.
Cemeteries dancing with blankets of burning
    candles, happy candles,
Lighting up the welcoming path for the dead.

Darkness of Loneliness
By John S. Culan

Loneliness is darkness consuming your heart
It is a desert sandstorm no one has seen

Loneliness is the burning woods
where no soul has ever been
no life has ever grown

It is a wolf howling in the woods
Loneliness is your shadow
disappearing in the shallow light

Loneliness is the deepest part of night

Jumping History
By Randy Hanson

History jumps on a trampoline,
doing summersaults and front flips.
He jumps into space like an astronaut going to
    Jupiter.
When he came back down,
a blustering cat was jumping, hissing and
    meowing.
It swallowed History and went on,
its tail waving back and forth like a pen writing
    fast.

Old White Shoe
By Mohamed Iman

An old white shoe
hangs on the telephone wire
and it is beautiful.
In the night
it's like a little star
and it gives a little bit of light
to the world.

The Gift
By Lizanne Koch

As I walked into my room
I saw that Buck, my cat,
Was standing on my bed.
A half-eaten, bloody lizard
Was on my pillow.

29

It was about a foot-and-a-half long.
I looked down at Buck.
He blinked affectionately.
Kneeling down, I patted him
On his striped orange head,
And his purr got even louder.
His wet nose pressed against mine.
An hour later, I had my dad
Dispose of the thing.
It was a wonderful gift.

The Horse of My Dreams
By Rachel Pack

The horse of my dreams
has spots like a sponge painting.
His eyes are dark as a thunder storm
and his feet graceful and strong.
His hair is beautiful as the springtime.
His sturdy legs shift side to side,
and he keeps watch as if someone was trying
to harm him. Rearing up, he seems as wild
as the weeds that grow around him.
He throws every man who tries
to ride him, because of the fear
and anger he smells inside them.
I know not to fear the horse,
but breathe with him,
becoming one within two.

The Kipah
By Caleb Rosen

I am on a kid's head
all day I hear waves crashing against the shore
he's so desperate to be in the ocean
the teacher cannot hear the desperation
if she could she would be amazed
she would say:
'why do I have to give this child homework?'
says the kipah on his head:
'please, let him go surf
it's giving me a headache
hearing the waves every day
crashing against the shore.'

Dust
By Katie Schmitt

I am Katie.
My family ignores me.
I am dust.
Nobody cares about me,
my hair as brown as chocolate,
my eyes big as erasers.
In Long Beach, where I was born,
my grandma's dogs chased me
because they didn't like me.
In the future I will not be dust.
I will be the stars
in the sky.

To a Mouse
By Meredith Snapp

You must have wriggled with joy
when you found that hole in the wall.
You must have squeaked with happiness
when you saw that cheese
on that wood block
like a platter all set out just for you.
How you must have run and
greedily bit into the cheese.
Then "POW!" the metal bar came down.
What a strange death: you lost your head,
but at the same time you got the cheese.
Have you learned your lesson now?

The Pencil Sharpener
By Lauren A. Susoeff

grinds my pencil
down to the eraser,

sits
and waits
to be fed
a banquet of pencils.

When someone feeds it,
it is a silver horse
being fed a carrot,

swishing its tail
around and around.

The Sea
By Julia Vazquez

At dusk,
the waves
hit the sunlight;
porpoises and fish
jump in the orange
of the sunset.

Herons fly through
the salty breeze,
hawks soar to the cliffs,
sea otters crack
their dinners
in the seaweed
and swim away.

The seals on the sand
not far from me
rest in a cave
touching the ocean.

The wind surges
and pebbles rattle.

I am alone.

Grade Six

Is It Wise to Live in Del Mar?
By Patrick Fay

No.
The tourists are as strange as snow in August.

They ask questions like,
"Where is the beach?"

They go to sleep at 6:30
to stay on Eastern Standard Time.

Tourists drive slowly and
look at maps while they drive.

This results in traffic jams from here
to New York. Maybe it is not wise

to live in Del Mar.

Seeing My Sister
By Maurisa La Chusa

Every day my little sister would climb the tree by
our house.

She could climb like a monkey without falling,
as fast as a lizard.
Her clothes were tight blue shorts,
big T-shirts and white high-tops.

She would climb into her room from the
  branches
and turn the radio
as high as she could, and dance.
Her room had the smell of roses.
On her light-brown dresser,
she had a crystal-clear bear and
a lot of stuffed animals.
She would climb that tree every day after school.
But now that she's gone,
I don't know what she does.
The walls are closing,
her dolls looking at me.

The Sea of Whispers
By Margaret Powell

As I walk past the raging sea
rough waves swell
a mad gust of wind
frowns and punches me in the back.

But I don't care.

I walk closer towards the sea
dip myself into the watery world.

The sea begins to whisper
Come, come with us.

The waves are like huge hands
taking me into their world.

Memory and Mind
By Arissa Rodriguez

Memory is a scar, permanent and stable
Memory is a newly discovered flower, beautiful
  and colorful.

Memory is a mustang, strong and fast.

Memory is a caramel apple
sweet on the outside
sour on the inside.

Memory is a mountain
you can't wait to get to the top.
Memory is a desert, harsh, empty
and thirsty for more.

Memory is a mom with baby pictures
and embarrassing stories.
Memory is pasta, good and long.

Memory is the only thing left of my grandpa.

Peace
By Katherine Najor

Peace is a relaxing feeling, like sipping warm hot
    chocolate on a cold winter day.
Peace is feeling relieved that the day's tasks are
    over.
Peace comes in a bright-eyed puppy gazing at you
    nose to nose.
Peace comes when taking off your slippers right

36

before you say your nightly prayers.
Peace is a feeling that comes when relaxing in a
hot bath filled to the brim with scented oils.
Peace is a feeling when you are asleep, and know
someone is taking care of you the rest of your
days.
Peace comes when a woman is gracefully sliding
her pen on canvas to make wonders.

Mystery Meat
By Dawn Vance

My mom was cooking something.
She wouldn't tell us what.
We couldn't go inside the kitchen
Or look into the pot.

She went to answer the telephone;
It was my grandma.
I decided to take a little look
And this is what I saw.

There was green stuff boiling over
And it smelled like old gym socks.
I found a book, a ring,
And a shoe inside the pot.

I leaned over to take a little sniff;
It almost knocked me down.
I pulled out an old basketball
And that's not all I found.

I found my missing earring

And my other eye contact.
I found my old homework
And a small box full of tacks.

I'm not going to eat that stuff.

I'd rather eat my feet.
My mom can make the weirdest things,
Especially mystery meat.

Grade Seven

Grandpa's Car
By Ignacita "Victoria" Archuleta

Car
sitting in the garage.
Old and rusted car,
my grandpa's car.
He used to drive it so slowly.
I look at the car sitting there,
think of my grandpa trying to get up,
looking at the car,
looking into my eyes.
I sit in the car
and remember when he used to hug me.

Rhythms
By Ayanna Arms

Something about dance
makes my toes tap
fingers snap
and body move.
I get vibes from the music.

When I dance
my heart beats
like the bass drums in the song.

Dance gets me movin'
like the old church ladies on Sunday mornin'.

39

Dance is life.
I float across the stage
like an angel floating quietly to Heaven.

When I dance
I feel like an apple in a lemon tree,
as I glide across the stage
all eyes are on me.

Power, by Sharilyn Shamlow

Confidential

By Lolly Beck-Pancer

The lady is my grandmother
Much is confined in her
The man by her side is my grandfather
He is impatient to leave
The girl standing between them is my mother
She is young and naïve

She knows nothing of his misdeeds
They are by the ocean
Waiting to swim
Once the photo is taken
The woman and her daughter
Will frolic in the water
'Till the sun is dim
While the man goes to the race track
To gamble his money away
When he returns the next day
He is drunk and depressed
The woman makes him coffee
The young child rests
They tell her nothing
For they want what is best for her
And hide this secret life . . .

A Child's Freedom, by Jackie Kennedy

La Niña del Pueblo
By Dulce Beltrán

Soy esa persona
que esta en el campo,
pensando en los animales
dandoles de comer,
me quieran o no.
Yo soy la misma,
la misma niña
que va caminando por ese pueblo
que tanto adoro.
Unos me quieren
otros no
pero eso no importa.
Solo importa como eres
tú por dentro de tu corazón
tus pensamientos
piensa en ti mismo.
Yo soy yo
dentro de mi
y seguire siendo la misma,
la misma niña del pueblo.

The Girl from the Country

I'm the girl
From the country
Who tends the animals,
Feeding them
Whether they love me or not.

I'm the same girl
Who walks

By the village
That I love so much.

There are those
Who love me,
Others who don't
But that doesn't matter to me.

All that matters is how you feel
In your heart,
Your thoughts
About yourself.

I remain myself.
Inside of me
I stay the same,
The same girl from the country.

Sombras Enojadas
By Fermin Borjon

Yo recuerdo cuando vivía con mi abuelita en
    Tijuana
que en un noche se oían cosas muy extrañas
como un hombre gritar.
También se oían niños llorar.
Todo esto pasaba en la media noche
cuando nadie andaba afuera en la calle.
Las sombras se miraban muy enojadas aquella
    noche.

Angry Shadows

I remember when I lived with my grandmother
   in Tijuana
that one night strange things were heard,
like the cry of a man.
Children were also heard crying.
All this happened in the middle of the night
when no one walks outside on the street.
The shadows looked angry that night.

The Essence of Light, by Emily Richards

She Told Me Not to Go
By Melanie Brophy

She told me not to go,
not to leave life so young.
She said it wasn't worth it.
I'm not so sure myself.
I guess Rosemary really cares.
I'm not so sure that I do, though.
They call me 'Psycho,'
like I'm a chained-up gorilla.
I guess I might be—
psycho, that is.
Nothing really means that much to me.
My friends tell me I need help,
but I tell them it's just depression,
hurricane clouds, spinning around me.
Others don't care as long as I stay away.

Swimming in Paper
By Heather Dowley

A book is like an ocean of words
I open my book and dive in
I swim through the pages
I am amazed at the characters
At their accomplishments
I swim deeper
I see places I never dreamed I'd visit
No shark can hold my imagination
In his razor-sharp teeth
Everywhere I swim I see golden riches
And threadbare rags
Mixed into a whir of color

I become the characters
Happy when they're happy
Sad when they're sad
The deeper I swim the better it becomes
Then comes the bookmark
My life preserver
Pulling me from the pages
Back to my own life
A book is like swimming
In the Sea of Cortez
during a hurricane . . .

War
By Solmaz Emami

The outside of a red pear is like war
with all of its red bloodshed,
cold and smooth on the outside
like a shiny new rifle.
Look inside a pear and it is white and pure,
innocent, like the men who go to war.
Inside they are not bad,
they only fight
for what they believe is right.
They only want to taste
the bitter-sweetness
of war
not knowing
that the crisp,
red, mean
exterior of
the pear
is
war.

Kiwi

By Irene Jimenez

The kiwi reminds me of war
The seeds are the soldiers
The green, the land
The only land with trees
The land they were fighting for
The green streaks represent the shootings
The white spot in the middle, the border
The border between the two territories
I can see one side winning
The side with more people
When the kiwi is squeezed, juice comes out
Juice that stands for water
Water trying to drown them
Telling them to stop the fighting
Now they are all buried under the land
The land with trees
The land they were fighting for.

Candle

By Jose Luis Sandoval

A high mountain
Sitting in a frozen lake.
In the top there is a bright tear blown by the
wind.

Eternity Is Too Short
By David McArthur

*inspired by "Partial view of a pit at the Bisham
Necropolis Archaeological
Exhibition—People's Republic of China*

They stand there, lifeless, motionless
But they have a mission
They stand in their pit of dirt
A world of gray gloom
Their bodies of clay are weaker than their souls
They carry clay weapons
that ward off an unseen foe
Some are decapitated, they do not care
They exist to protect a master long dead
They still remember everything
They allow the men of flesh and bone
To walk above them
They wait, pondering their purpose
Eternity is too short, they thought
When light touched them

Soul Music
By Matthew McIntosh

I believe that music
is the key to the soul,
like a door opening and squeaking,
the creaking sound of a rocking chair,
the ticking of the clock,
the swish
swish sound of the dishwasher.

Afghani Volcano
By Edrees Nassir

I come from Afghanistan.
I come from a country
where everyone worries about war.

A place where hunger
drought, sickness and death
is an everyday thing
like brushing your teeth.

A place where people
do not think about how
they look or what's in style
but how to make enough money
and if they'll survive until tomorrow.

Sometimes I feel like an erupting volcano
burning everything in its path
angry at people's selfishness
a wildfire burning until nothing's left to burn
yet sometimes I feel calm
a stream on a sunny day.

My life is like a kaleidoscope
not knowing what color, shape, or size
the next picture will be.

The Last Piece of Chicken
By Charlene Saint Clair

The last piece
of chicken on

the chicken bone
that nobody ate

will satisfy a
cat

which will feed
her baby kittens

that lie still
in a pair
of mittens.

Curiosity Keeps Calling
By Kristin Sammons

Pandora,
she follows me around the house.
She whispers to me, to open the box.
Curiosity sometimes wears a disguise
a long, black, hooded cloak.

She tells me to look through the mail
or listen in on someone's phone call.
I always recognize her voice
a blend of cackle and snicker
and I try not to listen.

When you look at curiosity
she smiles, not an ordinary smile
but rather a smirk or a grin
as if she is up to something.
She usually is.

Leaving
By Jenny Snow

He laughs, remembering a joke.
He tells us and we all laugh.

He pulls me up onto his lap,
and I turn to see his face,
but he blurs.

I remember him lifting me up,
threatening to drop me.
He's always playing.
The light shines upon his face,
lighting up his face.
He smiles up at me. We
laugh with joy, and I
give him a hug, then
go to my mother, and
then we leave.

We leave.
Always leaving.
Leaving my father.
Leaving my relatives.
Leaving my home.
Returning just to leave.
One side leaving, but
one side always staying.

I want my father to stay,
picking me up,
not always fading, blurring
when I turn to see him.

Road to Hope
By Emma Townsend-Merino

I come from
Spicy bean burritos
Eaten in a worn-out auto
Running out of Mexico
Without a second glance

Sweet apricots
Stolen from trees
Feeding the intense hunger
That comes from the long hours
Of picking fruit

Scalding Yuma, Arizona
A place to settle
Get a better job
Teach kids how
To speak English

Comforting albondigas
Eaten by a fire
Of stolen logs
While coyotes dance
In the moonlight

I come from
Weary travelers

Living on the edge of chaos
Until they came to lost liberty
America

Just a Petal
By Victoria Valdés

Before you were a petal you were a
seedling deep within the earth's core.
You were the sprout of hope in a deserted
garden. You were a source of entertainment
to a bored child. You were a gift of love.
You were an apology. You were the warmth
and only life to a grave. You were a decoration
placed in a vase. A stroke of color in a painting.
A sticker on a binder. A note between two
friends.
A secret of first love. You were the words to
"He loves me, he loves me not." You were
the wind blowing her tears away.

Loneliness, by Christina Bertrang

How to Reach Happiness
By Jeremy West

Don't go when in a bad mood. Go when the sun
   is shining
and the wet dew still fills the morning air. Look
up
through the trees of the forest to the rich blue
sky
lined with sweet stripes of white.
Close your eyes. Spin around and imagine
   paradise.
Think of something you love as you spin around
on the soft earth, twigs and fresh crisp grass
   cracking
beneath your feet. Untie the leash to your mind.
Let it wander as far as it wants to go.
That is how you reach true happiness.

Grade Eight

My Family
By Alison Angione

My sister is a rotten apple,
never sweet, always sour,
the real her, anyway.

My parents are divorced.
They are like oil and water;
they don't mix
and are rarely
t o g e t h e r.

My horse is a wild spirit
blazing over every obstacle
with her fiery pace.

I'm a black spot on a white carpet
dark and quiet, just there, mysteriously
insignificant.

Jazz Cat, by Hilary Kearney

Answers from the Mountain
By Jared Bird

Climb the tall, tall mountain
get to the summit
I can see the whole land before me
I get down on my knees
ask which god is right for me
pray for an answer
I wait for the reply
and then it comes
the words come rolling out of the dark clouds
they echo across the land
loud booming voices
I hear them all
Why can there be so many?
How can all of them be right?

What It's Not
By Emily Boost

The white soap sits
in a soap dish in my bathroom.
Easily it slips through my fingers
just like this poem slips through my mind.
The sudsy little bubbles remind me of my
    emotions:
transparent and delicate, they are easily
    broken.
One by one they disappear from view,
and I feel the pain coming.

My hands come up to my face,
washing the tears off my cheeks.

56

I'm not crying because I'll miss you,
   although I will.
I'm not crying because I love you,
   although it's true.
I'm crying because I'm sorry.

It's all in the past now that I
know.
But I can't help it.
You forgave me without the ex-
planation you
   deserved.
I didn't mean to hurt you.
I didn't want to make you cry:
I just wanted you
to love me.

Dog Tags of a Fallen Hero,
by Brandon Schlegel

Don't Tell
By Oscar Burakoff

I am a dork. I'm no fun.
I don't like to play with anyone.
Salty tears on my cheeks
tell me I'm a dork.
I wrap myself in my arms
and realize I also wear glasses.
I didn't brush my hair today.
I'm a dork.

I had a dream I couldn't fly.
Like running into a stone wall,

57

my dream was weird,
a mystery with no light.
I couldn't spread my wings
to get over the wall.
And I am that bird, struggling
with my problems, wanting
liberation from the darkness of life.

After the dream fractured my life,
it all came back together.
My face was nice. I was wearing a robe
but I had nothing to conceal.
Now I know that I'm only
what I think of myself.
I'm no dork anymore.
I still wear glasses. Sometimes
I don't brush my hair. But I won't
tell anyone about what I learned.

Seatbelts, Please, by Elena Monroe

Basketball
By Orlando Casinio

Round, bouncing
like the world
in the palms of your hands.
Sounds like the beating
of a drum,
like the wind
on a cool day.
When you hold it in your hand
it feels like you are as strong
as ten men.

Masks Abstract
By Leslie Crews

This dying rose
is like my grandmother,
wilting away . . .
yet not quite gone,
warmth
still radiating
from the center
but ready to float away
on the wind.
The endless stairway
winds up into
the deepest peace of mind.
You know
something
someone
has to be there;
you can just reach it,
winding up the stairs,

but the stairs never
stop winding.
The person
is there
somewhere,
yet hiding,
like a child,
behind the dark,
brittle doorway of petals.

There's Time for Math Tomorrow
By Jessica Fink

Yesterday I said
"I'll do my math project tomorrow"
Tomorrow is today
I need to:
research the origin
of triangles
calculate the weight
of a feather
draw pie charts
of government funds
discover
the 5th dimension
never mind
I don't know the 4th
Use the Quadratic Equation
to carefully measure
how long time travel takes
and while I'm at it
I need to cube root

a cube disguised as a rectangle
measure the length
of my middle name
in centimeters
millimeters and decimeters
compute the circumference
of my milk glass
write the next
distance/time formula
and much more
I will do it
Like I said...Tomorrow...

The Thin Line Between Man and Beast,
by Dana Ung

Coral
By Heather Grant

My mother is like coral, living vibrant in the sea
Her heart has a vast gap in the center
Trying to suck in love
Yet it only escapes
Her spirit is rough as sand
Yet smooth as silk
She has built walls around herself
For her own protection
She has anger like a volcano
Ready to burst
But she holds it in
Like clouds hold rain
Her feelings are bumpy
Like craters on the moon
Yet she tries to smooth them out
As if ironing
She is like an eye about to open
With something keeping it shut
So as not to see the ugliness of the world
She is like a soft textured cookie
That can become hard in an instant
She is like an island floating in the middle of
    the sea
All alone, yet seemingly happy with a smile on
    her face
She loves and cares for us as a mother should
Yet my mother is like coral dying in the sea

Lao-tzu
By Michael Hoang

A wise man you are
Your wisdom goes beyond Confucius
Your teachings are simple
Yet few understand
Generals knew and feared your wisdom
So they sent dancing girls and fine horses to
  your prince
To corrupt him
Kings tried to understand your teachings
One misinterpreted them, and burned all the
  books of China
Your greatness was shunned by the
  communists
Confucius is of the light
You are of the dark
But light becomes dark
Dark becomes light
Nothing stays still for long
Light means life
Dark means death
In life something dies
In death something will be born.

Only Time Will Tell, By Alicia Martinez

Snowboard Love
By Sheri Kurisu

Snowboarding is love.
Both are unexpected
and intertwined.
You stand at the top
and look down
at the slope beneath you.
The thought, "Should I?" crosses your mind.
In relationships, there is certainty as well.
Going down a nice, easy slope
is fun, relaxing and enjoyable.
But then, all of a sudden
you're going too fast
and you can't stop!
Before you know it, you're saying "I do"
as you kiss the fresh, white snow.
But what have you gotten yourself into?
You're stuck and stranded with no way out.
The ride is no longer smooth and fun.
It's cold and harsh and hurts you.
You wish it could be good again,
but you don't see what went wrong.
You have nowhere to turn
so you cry out for help.
Then another love comes by
and brushes off the harshness and hurt.
You both go back to the top
of the slope and start the journey
of love all over again.
This is snow boarding and love.

A Face with a Heart, by Tina Utter

Apparent Shapes and Colors
By Ramil Legaspi

Waiting, sitting down,
I gaze out the window,
my only choice of entertainment.
I watch the leaves rustle
as they push past,
the wind forcing them to dance.
As I sit, my world rushes past at great speed.
Trees run backwards and blend into one green,
anxious and bored altogether.
Colors turn to shapes, shapes to
separate colors.
The apparent wind fades, and I feel warm.
My world is still.
I feel joy arriving.

Family Collage
By Amber Malaney

I am a flower
blossoming in a shade of beautiful orange
standing shy in the corner.

My younger sister is a heart
holding our family together.
She is the center of our family.

My mother is the sun
shining down on us
with bright sincerity and concern.
She blinds us with her light.

My older sister is a cloud
floating farther away.
Faster and faster she goes,
never looking back.

My father is a mountain
standing proud and tall.
He reaches out to my sister,
but never gets close.

Adam's Hands
By Daniel McLean

Adam's small delicate hands
are beaded with sweat and shaking with delight
at the wonder around him.
The huge toy store fills his vision
and his hands shake harder.

They shake like San Francisco
in the earthquake.
"Why are your hands shaking?" I ask him.
With euphoric light
shining in his eyes, he tells me:
"The toys are talking.
They are talking to me!"

Don't You See?
By Naomi Geraci

Don't you see?
At school,
Shields are up.
Every day from seven to two,
We hide
Even among friends.

Don't you see
The difficulty of a good poem?
To reveal enough to be "real"
Is to risk exactly what we work all day to avoid:
Utter embarrassment.
The word must be just right
Not "too" anything.
Not too serious, not trying too hard to be funny
Not too emotional, not pretentious
Not too personal, not phony
Not too teacher-pleasing
But pleasing enough for everyone.
In other words,
Perfect.

Don't you see?

Even the popular elite
Pretending
Maybe more than anyone else.
Today, punks sit in a perfect row
Matching black t-shirts
Bobbing spiked heads in unison
Listening to "Fat Lip":
"I don't want to be
A casualty of society."
Who sees the irony?
We don't want to be trapped
In this web of pretending
But it's survival
And we're mostly happy
Until we have to write poetry.
Don't you see how much you're asking?

Equality at School?
By Elke Nash

At school they teach us equality.
We pledge allegiance to our flag,
the red, the white, the blue
that symbolize everyone's freedom
for him, for her, for you
not just for one, but for all.

In a place where equality is the law,
segregation is practiced by blacks,
by whites, by all.

In classrooms, we discuss our law.
We argue for our rights
in the land of the free,
the home of the brave.

68

School is where we learn to fight.

We unite in class,
we stand as one,
but at lunchtime we divide.
We morph into groups
by race, by color, by choice.

Here is America's future,
here are America's rights,
but here is where we start splitting
and forgetting they're everyone's rights.

Sidewalk Lost
By Michael Oliver

Leaves crackle under my brand new white
shoes.
The trees stare and laugh at me. When I look
up at
the trees whispering their secrets, the sun
shines in my eyes.
I try to get away, look elsewhere, but the sun fol-
lows me,
staring at me.
Like a beam of lightning, my family flashes
before my eyes.
I kneel down to tie my lace. The leaves are still.
Instead,
my bones crackle and break until I pile up on
the sidewalk.

Black

By Nancy Rodriguez

Black is
the color
of death.
Black is
the color
of the
night, running
through the
lines that
divide us
and Mexico.
The color
reminds me
of innocent
people running
for a
fake fantasy
that will
never be
true.

Blue Anger

By Veronica Wilson

A tree
shedding its leaves
sat
hoping for peace
from the hard
blue wind.

Grade Nine

Smiling Jack
(The Ripper's Reflection)
By Diana Chaudron

As a child, I was ridiculed
For my deformity.
And now in my death,
I walk the streets of modern London,
A murderous specter.
If I returned,
I would host a macabre Mardi Gras
Celebrating my 300th anniversary.
They never discovered the face behind the masks.
And I, the consummate actor,
Excelled at creating illusion.
In the foggy East End
You can still trace my steps
On the slick cobblestone.
My reverie ended, but not by choice.
As I disappear
Into the mists of time,
Mockeries of myself
Still live on.
Copycats who paint in blood
Commemorate my legacy
Until they themselves are dust.

Popcorn
By Jenny Feng

A golden droplet of water
tumbles and drops.
When joined by others,
its perfection multiplies
into a field of blooming white roses.

A Wave
By Ray Gonzales

My mother
is like a wave

always unpredictable
there at times

gone when you need her
she doesn't know

the pain
she can inflict

always crashing
with full might

always rippling into the sand
always repeating until
the ocean is still

Only What It Wants
By Sarah Merchant

She's dark and smiling.
The bandanna that holds her
hair allows her earrings to dangle.
Her eyebrows are raised and she
laughs. Her arms are thrown out and
from one a watch shines. Her
tank top reveals only what it
wants to and she laughs. Her
legs are crossed comfortably. The
plant shines sun and an uneven
pattern that a glass of water
makes on the sill. The radio hides
behind her and she laughs. She
will laugh forever here because
it's black and white here and
she laughs.

Monolith, by Joaquin Tena

Sky of Dreams
By Richard Ramos

I dream of many things
not one, not two, but many things.
I have a sky of dreams.
Each star is like a wish
and there are many stars in the sky.
But no matter how many stars there are
when the sun comes up, they go away.

The Burned Doll
By Jessica Trail

One eye shut more
than the other
missing fingers
missing toes
burned-up face
burned-up everywhere
Eyes not sparkling
hair not shiny
dress full of ash
shoes full of holes
My grandma gave
me this burned doll
to show me you don't
always have to spend
money to get something
beautiful

I Used to Be

By Heather Trumbull

I used to be small,
but now I'm tall.

I used to be dumb,
but now I'm smart.

I used to be lost,
but now I'm found.

I used to be afraid,
but now I'm brave.

I used to be weak,
but now I'm strong.

I used to hate to write,
but now I love to write.

I used to hate,
but now I love.

I used to be poor,
but now I'm rich.

Rich of love, strength, and fulfillment
because I know that my mother, sick
as she may be, is still there for me.

Funny Tongue, Sad Eyes
By Lynn Uhazle

He thinks he's funny
As he sticks his tongue out
Way out
As far as it will go
Out to his chin.

And his friend takes a picture.

But I know he's not funny
Because his eyes are not funny.
They have no expression.
They are almost sad.

But he thinks he is acting funny.

Mother
By Kris Ybarra

My mother
is a burning fire
her presence can mean
comfort and warmth
or warped skin

pain and protection
can come from the
same source

tragedy occurs
when the flames leap
and wreak havoc on
their surroundings

the chain of fire
is hard to stop
from eating house after house
leaving only burnt shells

I need water

Grade Ten

A Walk Through the Neighborhood
By Ari Brown

At my house,
    monotony dwells.
I walk down the path
    to where traffic
      and excitement live.
Neatly manicured plants

lawns that need cutting.

A right turn onto Adams;
no more neat houses,
    businesses now.
Kensington Coffee Co.
    packed with people,
the smallest library
    on earth.

I walk in the noontime sun,
    block on block.
      Fairmont, Mission Gorge,
they fall away from
      tired shoes.

Past the hospital,
    Kaiser Permanente,
a parking lot grown
    fat on pain;
death goes there to have fun.

I pass the statue
    big and bronze.
It shines in the afternoon's
    dying light.
I twist my way
    through the lost streets,
down unknown paths,
        wrong ways, no outlets,
the cul-de-sac, always a mystery.
Streets are meant
      to go somewhere . . .

I round the corner,
    find some shade.

Two people emerge
    from the shadows
yelling at each other;
what they say is not important.

Nothing ever works
    in their world.

The Tumbler, by Allen Isabelo

To Be in Love with a Leaf
By Tidiane Diallo

The leaf swaying in the breeze
Like the hair of a beautiful girl
Soft and light
Dancing in the wind
Color on her face
Like the colors of fall
Her body curves
Like the leaf
Like a flame
Like a mountain
Everyone wants to climb
To see a view
Of the shimmering stars
A perfectly shaped leaf
Fragile and delicate
Every time I talk to her
I get nervous and act like a fool
In love, that's what I am
Soon, I too will become a leaf
In the hair of a beautiful girl

Secret

By Julia Fulmer

Soft, white, and misshapen
Her tired, aching hands sprinkle tiny seeds—
new life over the soil.
Her fingers are bent
and look as though they will wither away
like the dead weeds she tosses aside.
There is something in her hands, in their past
that is a mystery to me—
I am too young.

One Stormy Evening, by Maggie Mittelsteadt

My City, by Christian Cardona-Glizondo

I Am a Star
By Lisbeth Luna

I am a star.
I can be bright or dark.

When I'm bright
I am a diamond ring that
everybody wants to wear.

When I'm dark
I am a dark closet that
nobody wants to enter.

Tragedy at Night, by Denise Lubanga

The One Who Is
By Natalina Reda

I am the one
Set from discrimination
Loving the skin that I am in
With the strut in my walk
And the tone of my talk
I am the one
The one who will make a difference
No more white this or black that
The one to stop the chit chat
I am the one
To make my color known
Screaming and yelling to the crowd
I am black and proud

The one to stop the drugs
With their dark and soulless cries
And the one to stop crime
And create a golden taste of time
I am the one
With burning eyes of agony and defeat
Because the time I have left is all too weak
I am the one
The one who has a secret
Not thinking a soul could keep it
I also am the one who is
Strong in sight with anger and might
The one who is, is me
I'm glad I know who I can be
But the real question is
"Can you be you?"
Or imitate what isn't true.

Grade Eleven

Reflection
By Jenny Bengen

The parlor was quiet
except for whispers which rustled around the
   room
like leaves in autumn.
I was seven, Grandma was dead.
Slowly I crept forward, wanting to see
Mother's mother.
There—her face was peace.
Reaching out, I softly pressed my finger to her
   cheek
and stared in shock at what came off.
It was thick, pasty, and bronze.
My blood rushing, I hurriedly wiped it off on
   her collar.
There—a screaming spot of orange upon her
   dress.
I retreated to my seat, wondering what I had
   taken away.

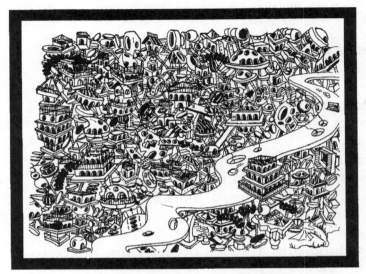

My House, by Lisa Kingery

Sun in Florence
By Laura Brenneman

I have never seen your hands,
but I have felt their touch.
Your smooth script unfolds across a page
like a warm blanket on a child grown cold.
I wrap myself in the words.

It has been four summers since I have seen the
    sun in Florence.
The heat coursed through stone streets
    and up radiant colonnades,
turning them to gold.
Jagged edges softened as liquid eyes moved
    towards the center,
the cathedral,

86

strung on a organ's cedared perfume.
Four years since I longed, unabashed, to lie
in the faded satin of the
domed hope chest,
and watch every note slide against the rounded
    walls.

An aria of color rained beyond stained glass
as ebbing sun shifted white embers
and you turned to approach me.

Now you write letters
peppered with questions of my world.
Do you want to see the jagged edges?

Gnawed with unsettling hunger,
I draw your words from their cedared chest.
I am moved to pull away the heavy lid
and reveal a spiral of webbed fingers.
Notes from a forgotten score,
left to lull and resound in buried folds,
    as wild aster,
gasping beneath the leaden cloak of the moor,
long to lie in the sun.

You were shrouded in the light of a cathedral,
and I did not know you.
But as the glove unravels, I see the tense
    muscles of our palms.
And I cannot let you go, your grasp is so strong.

The Letter

By Kathleen Halberg

I have a letter
      one written by my father
          to me.

It was written on a sad day
      in a forbidden room.
With an IV in his arm
      he wrote the letter to me
      with strong scarred hands
      that were weak with pain.

His hands, left uneven and incomplete
by a thirsty man with a gun.

He confessed his love to me
      by writing

"I cannot wait
      to see you
          to hold you
      and to cry with you."

This, his statement of his love,
      is worth more to me that
      all the love in the world.

It stays visible in my room
      and reminds me of the father
      I used to have.

Above a Winter Freewayscape,
by Michael Nelson

Grandfather
By Kelly Halligan

I never really knew him,
but in a way I did.
He was my grandfather,
but not really.
He lived a block away and never visited.
I had a vision of what he was like:
he was a police officer,
or a pilot,
or even a fireman.

But I knew I was wrong.
I knew what he really was:
a mean old man with no occupation,
living with his various wives and cats.
And yet he was alone,
always alone.
It was strange when he finally died.
It was as if my emotions were still,
awaiting a command.
Should I be upset?
Should I cry?
Should I be relieved or glad?
I didn't know.
So I went to my room,
closed the door,
and turned up the music.

Ridley Road
By Amy Montierth

I have no idea
what love is,
so I'll stick with infatuation.
Beauty?
It's nothing,
nothing I can see,
and Fear is an inescapable as my shadow.

Comezón de Paz

By Anacelly Quintana

Me da comezón en mi corazón para ir al bosque
y
vivir en una casa hecha de adobe donde uno
puede llegar a pie
con los árboles grandes como un gigante
y el camino lleno de tierra y peidras.
La casa enterrada como un poro en la tierra
durmiendo y
hay paredes con curves de una cebolla.
Descansando de la gente ocupada
con las pensamientos de las ciudades del
mundo.

The Itch for Peace

My heart itches to go into the wilderness,
to live in an adobe house
where my feet can lead me on walks
through trees as big as giants
on a rocky dirt road.
The house's doorway will be like a pore
        in the face of the sleeping earth,
the walls with curves like an onion's.
A place resting from people busy
with thoughts of the cities around the world.

My Grandfather
By Trisha Esquivel

Hard and strong, my grandfather is the rock.
His skin is dark and smooth
with soft wrinkles, a gift from time.
He is of the earth, and the earth of him.
His body is bent over from the work
in his garden. I never tasted better
    watermelon,
so full and ripe. His hands are stained
from the sienna earth he toiled upon
his body pained. The lines in his hands run
    deep
with stories of the lake we looked
out at from the decaying pier we used to fish
    from.
They are like the long road of his life,
his blood running through his worn body
a river cutting the land.

Grade Twelve

The Melody of a Memory
By Summer Clardy

The room was dim
except for candles
It was raining outside
and he played for me
singing me to sleep
as he did when I was younger
It brought back memories
and fear of the future
It made me cry
but he did not notice
and his image flickered in and out of focus
like the candle's dancing flame
and you could see the emotion in his eyes
He was filled with his song
as the room was filled with its sweet melody
and my eyes filled with tears of pain and confusion
all something he would never remember
and I could never forget

Soy el Viento
By Francisco A. Hernández

Soy el viento
que navega alrededor,
sin final y sin termino,
estoy ahí, siempre,
dándote vida.

Soy la fuente de energía
de remolinos de dulce,
y los niños me usan para volar sus papelotes.
Soy vida,
la crueldad de la gente.
Soy el viento,
el inmigrante sin visa,
Toco a todos,
nadie me mira.
Muchos me odian,
muchos me admiran.

I Am the Wind

I am the wind
that rides all around
true, and without end.
I am there always,
giving you life.
I am the energy
of the candy windmills,
and the kids use me to fly their kites.
I am life,
the cruelty of people.
I am the wind,
the immigrant without a visa.
I touch everyone,
but no one sees me.
Many hate me,
and many admire me.

Strangers Met in Moonlight,
by Maly Oudommahavanh

My Dearest Buddha
By Max Krashow

Sitting
Silent
Eyes closed in meditation
Is how I found you
My Buddha
My would-be
Could-be
Couldn't-be lover

95

Teacher
Friend   and
Key

So many years I spent
At your side
Fawning
Yearning for your touch
Your benediction
With you I seemed so close
Almost in your arms
In your head and heart
If only
Only I was fooled
Fooled by your nature
It wasn't out of malice
And I harbor no regret
As I hope you do not as well
We were both mistaken
Fooled by gimmick
By substance
Where existence should have been
By loneliness
When we should have been alone
And happy

Even now
As I turn my back
Not on you
But on my projection
Misconception of you
I cringe in doubt and fear
Of letting go of life
And love
And all the beauty I saw in you

All my misconceptions
Of the true nature
Of the Buddha

Ice

By Bryan Ludwig

Encased in a Lucite block,
frozen forever in time,
a beast locked in a clear cold coffin,
a scorpion caught in ice.

Claws frozen outstretched
tail curved, ready to attack.
Legs forever scrambling,
he's forever still.

Closed tight in a box,
the little beast isn't so bad.
Yet to meet him in the open,
scuttling swiftly across the sand
is painful:
he's a poison too potent to bear.

A scorpion in my memory
frozen like my mind.
That beast
of a stepparent
who has lost all
his power over me,
is now encased,
frozen forever, poised to attack,
and at the tip
of his colored tail,
a brief, black stinger.

Nobody Special
By Tim Tran

To children at recess, I am the fat kid
the one who throws the teamball the hardest.
To my mother, I am the natural-born leader
expected one day to abolish taxes on groceries.
In retrospect, I am neither.
I don't create masterpieces like Monet
or invent new names for hamburgers.
But I am present, like acres of blue grass
swaying in the rapture of a burning savannah.
I am a child among wolves that wait at every
    corner
to see if I am the one who wears
the red hood.

Shattered
By David Wright

A young man stands at his window,
Looking.
His faint reflection,
The person he thinks he is,
Shatters,
And for a brief moment,
He is lost
In a white blur,
Crashing to the ground,
In a million pieces.
But when he looks up
He realizes
The world outside,

Is clearer than ever before.

Phoenix, By Daphne San Jose

Poet-Teachers

Yes, there's laughter, but it can also break your heart . . .

The men and women who teach poetry in the schools can party with the best of them: wine-tinged celebrations follow the annual fair, with midnight humor on a sea-scented balcony and fond recollections of the year just past . . . look, over there! aren't the poet laureate's cheeks getting AWFULLY rosy? And . . . oh my . . . it's nice to see the prize-winning lady artiste letting her hair down so DECISIVELY on this warm Spring night . . . (who's her driver?)

All good clean fun . . . but the years pass, and all these young poets are human, and they age and . . .

It is shocking, every time, when one of this small group of poet-teachers passes away.

Over the years, two poet-teachers have died— Jim Allen of a heart attack in 1998 and, much more recently, Claudia Axel of breast cancer*.

As I write this, I'm looking at the picture of Claudia that appeared in the 2002-2003 Border Voices booklet. She looked so young. She WAS so young, with her long curly hair, bright smile, unlined cheeks. The booklet says that Claudia "invites students to celebrate the extraordinary in their everyday lives," and that she uses "music, visual and performing arts and meditation" to help kids write.

When I think of Claudia and the sadness of her early death, I remember a poem she wrote before the awful diagnosis came down, a remarkable poem called "Wisteria." It's a lovely bit of writing, made more wondrous by the fact that, read today, it seems to offer consolation to those who loved her, as if the poet had somehow known that death was near, and then had turned, and looked at all the wonderful things she had created in her life, and embraced them and asked us to do the same. Listen:

See what I have created from my strength
purple strings of flowers strung together . . .
      . . . with a scent   so light it
Will make you fly—

. . . Today I am here and if you want
if you want   you can
catch this sun flickering through me ...

in the glorious seamlessness
of this breathing
moment.

Elsewhere in this book I've described how important the Border Voices poets are for our kids, how their work results in significant increases in test scores as well as a deeper understanding of the Self. This section of the book has a different purpose: to let readers get acquainted with a remarkable group of people in the best way possible — through their poetry.

You will find Claudia's poem in the next few pages, as well as poems by other poet-teachers past and present, some full of laughter, all worth reading.

Go on now. They're waiting for you . . .

Wisteria
By Claudia Axel

All winter your winding branches like muscular
          arms encircled
poles branches shaded
overhang in brown
grey trunk.
But today—spring—you sing a different song:

See what I have created from my strength
purple strings of flowers strung together
bent towards the earth
yet   with a scent   so light it
Will make you fly—

a few days—a week maybe
my blossoms will be gone and
I will work again
but now I live
in the glory of purple love   my gift
to myself and whomever will accept
this flight of delicacy
that comes from strength

Today I am here and if you want
if you want   you can
catch this sun flickering through me   I will

sweep you to your senses   give you the peace
       of Light
Catch me   catch me   I will show you your
body I
will hold you up and I
will give you the luxury of
every nightmare erased
in the glorious seamlessness
of this breathing
moment.

The Sign
    By James D. Babwe

That was me with the sign
by the side of the road
standing close to the far west end
of Interstate 10.

It read:
Arizona or Nevada
or The Other Coast — I Don't Care
when summer was time
for rolling down windows
and thunderstorm air,
lightning in the giant sky —
cruising past field after field
on the flat side of Colorado,
where corn grows
tall and sweet and blonde.

Mile after mile,
racing fast through Kansas and Nebraska,
I watched wheat wave and whisper
in the warm wind.

I caught an Oklahoma look
at a seven pound steak,
saw a three-headed snake
on the outskirts of Amarillo,
ate Mississippi grits with a stack of pancakes,
veered north to Vermont,
carved a path through mountains
and granite mines in Maine,
stuck my toes in the ocean
off the New Jersey coast,
caught up on current events in real places
         called
Cheesequake and Quaxton
before barreling south to Atlanta,
where I took a hard right
to Texas and New Mexico —
stuck a thumb in the air (pointed west)
got picked up and rode on a busload
of dentures and canasta
on a heavily medicated tour
all the way to Las Vegas.

I fried my skin red
in the blazing hot sun,
swayed on my feet
when I got shoved
by the rush of the wind
from big double trailers
on a Carolina-California run,
and in case you didn't hear me say
thanks for the ride — thanks for the ride.

That was me with the sign
by the side of the road

standing close
to the far west end
of Interstate 10,
and the more I think
about people I've met
and places I've been,
the more I want
to see them again.

That was me
with the sign
by the side of the road.

That was me
with the sign
by the side of the road.

es cribir for you
por Francisco Bustos
By Francisco Bustos

es cribir

is what i meant
por ver
vision
en aquel instante
when i reached
out
for us
y entonces
nosotros
saw
todo
once y para

siempre
again
la luz esa
which
you bring
contigo

muse gracias
por tus sueños
and those seeds
siempre there

gracias . . .
always

Museum Vessels
for Thurman Statom
  By Brandon Cesmat

On a ledge in earthquake country,
vases vibrate with students' ideas.
In museum light, prisms divide into
    corn yellow survival,
        royal freedom of words,
            violet depth of smiles.
An afternoon slivered so students can carry
        visions away.
What revolves with vestiges of the glassblower's
        breath?
As vases swell with all that flows past
        their open lips,
which voices of awe make their vacancies

vibrantly quiet?

When I Come Back
By Glory Foster

I want to be a hummingbird
like the one my son saved in a matchbox
for over a year. Its ruby throat,
green forked-tail and sides
shimmering in its tiny bed.

To be an aerial acrobat
flashing color, quick as light
lost in the forgetfulness of perfume
as I am lost carrying words from my brain
as if it were pollen on my beak
propagating flowers, enflaming language.

To take up so little space, that I am lighter
than the question asked yesterday,
"Do we live again?"
To live with doubt or fly backward,
drunk on nectar and sun.
To travel from the Arctic to the Equator
in one season my heart beating in wonder
as ant-like buffalo herds graze
and the river's veins drain
the mountain's throat.
To sleep in the night's slow torpor,
to feel my feathers tune to the Earth's tilt,
and the sun's flight chill my hollow bones.

And then to return to the Big Sur coast

108

where cougars stalk mule deer
where honeysuckle and wild roses perfume
        the air.
And where I will end my days
in some boy's pocket
lost among stones and caterpillars,
a remnant of feathers and air.

Ode to The Bay*
   By minerva (Gail Hawkins)

Creativity is childhood visited.
Who you are is answered.
It began in San Francisco
when I walked up
the hills knees bent.

That's the wrong way to do it
a San Franciscan told me.
Then the city changed
and I took hop-scotch steps.
A writer who becomes a teacher
loves her students
and the Bay.

I walk up hills with legs straight now.
I am a tall woman.
Determined to return
to the hills and pages of it all.

The bookstores and hair salons
of East Coast blacks.
Ghirardelli chocolate indeed.

The pages turn and go
up each visit. BART
rides put me one foot
in my Philadelphia hometown.
Reminded by architecture
of Oakland and late night
poetry readings in the Haight.

Fog and tree leaves rock me
back to palms, beach and sun
as the Southland state home base
San Diego prepares me
for the hunger of another
Golden Gate, beautiful place.

Think and be gone.

The Talents I Didn't Get
By Jackleen Holton

came disguised as dreams,
each one a rare bird that flew
from the empty cup of my hands.

In all, there were too many to count.

Like a gaggle of popular girls
who snickered as I stumbled

from pink ballet slippers,
they were impossible to befriend.

They had names like Melody and Grace.

And once I'd exhausted all
the common arenas: track,
theatre, basketball court,

I developed a knack, I daresay even
a talent, for spotting new
and exotic venues for failure.

Case in point: synchronized
swimming. For two years I flapped
about like a caught fish, gasping
for air, swallowing water.

At regionals, I lost my nose plug
on the second backward tuck. My hair
raveled free of its gelatined bun.

The talent for knowing when to call
it quits: another of the numerous
gifts I wasn't bequeathed.

Even now when I lie in bed,
flinging hopeless arrows
at sleep, I can see them gliding
in figure-eights above me, uncatchable
sparks flying from the blue
ribbons of their wings.

Water & Bloom
By Georgette M. James

A mother travels
from one country
to another.
Her son follows.
Exactly how far
he cannot say.

Even still he recalls
pine trees yielding
to *agaves* and *zapotes*,
the clattering of heels
across cobblestone
and church bells chiming
upon the hour.

Even now he can taste
the warm *churros*
and *chocolate caliente*
in the early morning haze
and see the old men
hunched over dominoes
in the plaza at dusk.

Think of a boat
navigating a river.
How much belief
does it take to keep
a child afloat?

The boat navigates
on love, you say.
The perils vary

yet the water
remains the same.

Think of the unseen gifts
contained in a word
or in an embrace,
of the purple bougainvillea
bursting into flame.

Divorce

By Roxanne Kilbourne

In the howl of insanity
Children smile on cue
Dance freely
In circles of summer memories
Avoid the triangle of our disparities
Laugh
To lure us back
To lost treasures
Where we might once again
Stand by a river's edge
Glance at our reflections
And love again

Monarchs*

(a true story, NYC, Ground Zero, 2001)
   By Seretta Martin

Search dogs lead firemen
through a thick air,
wretched with the stench of death.

Streets are heavy laden
with fallen walls, lamp posts
buried in mounds of plaster,
lights blown out.

Mind-weary, yet they trudge
with hope of finding
another breath.

As if someone calls them,
the men look up, see a tower
of light; a flock of butterflies
hovers and descends
through hellborn dust.

One, golden with welkin wings,
rests on a fireman's shoulder.

"Souls," he whispers —
and the men bow in prayer.

---

* From *Foreign Dust Familiar Rain, New and Selected Poems* by Seretta Martin.

114

Exuviating Light
By Jim Milner

Fall fires took my home.
27 years on the mountain
skirted by dense chaparral
under old oaks and leaf-light.
Late afternoons, umbrage of oak
leaves splayed across our living room
walls — a network of twigs, leaves, wind;
terpsichore of shadow and light; a room
for one leaf to enter, settle in the mind
        an effigy.

Does this leaf now shed
its light always;
will light ever
be the leaf's to shed;
or does light shed the leaf
in passing?
These questions:
essential, futile, both?

My wife, Galen, dead now nine months —
consumed at night by the light of fire —
her hair brittle as dried leaves,
on her back, beginning bridge pose
full face to a burning sky.

When I found her body, I placed one
hand on her forehead, another
on her chest
and tried to say goodbye;
I stood and stumbled and
dropped, shoving my hands

into still-warm earth
blackened with ash,
screaming her name
over and over
as if I could call her from
out of this burnt ground.

And now I find myself
in a place of greened leaf-light,
half-shade,
moving and sitting,
air cool and easeful
in my throat.
I hardly can tell
if I pass here under these leaves,
under this sky,
or if they are slipping through me —
their light, the light's leaves,
burn now forever.

The Beijing Bell Temple
On a Line by C. Milosz
By Joe Milosch

I

There exists in Beijing a Temple of Bells.
The slim caretaker smiles as she will
behind the counter of miniature bells.
When she believes the temple is empty,
she plays a melody so sweet the birds
gather in elliptic circles to listen as her
wooden mallet strikes softly the iron bells.

116

I sit out of view as the tune she phrases
employs concrete benches and brass bells
to conjure the memory of the appearance
of Northern Lights as grandfather and I
fished south of Brief Bay. Whenever
he caught a fish, he'd say, "Some we toss
back and others we eat." In Bejing I wonder
how a mechanic with a third grade education
paraphrased Marcus Aurelius, and realized
knowledge does not require a belief in heaven
or hell, or a labyrinth of philosophy to exist.

II

Rocking in my patio chair, I listen to chimes
and return to the Bell Temple where I rode
the waves of the Bell Master's Melody.
Memories of the slender musician
in her olive dress along with memories
of an island where the sunrise acts
as a bugle call for swarms of mosquitoes
to hover above the rabbit's carcass.
During the day, sound seemed to die
at the drip line of a cluster of beech trees.
At sunset, sound gained strength enough
to echo inside hollow logs, to uncloak foam
rustling along the shore, and to allow fish
to splash water in search of game. All this
appeared normal to the fishermen, who listened
as they watched the aurora borealis and
found quietude in the wilderness within.

For Lucía
By Nicholas Moramarco

this is the silence of distance and closeness
through words
fingers
across land wires wind time sense motion
into now
only now
where new life constantly surprises us with her
delicate wisdom
and always coming light

it's not what might be
but what is that hums a soft tune into your ear
when you let it: smile, embrace this something
while surfing gracefully towards the horizon
of wordless sunsets and things unknown

The trunk
By Jill Moses

A black metal trunk with silver latches
sits on my chest
full of bird feathers, handkerchiefs
and hearts of stone.
It is your trunk, father
the one you carried up the stairs
from the garage
to lock up your hair tonic and socks
because your son used a few drops
without your permission.
Stingy man, I carried this weight for years

118

until I abandoned the trunk in a parking lot,
    unopened.
The parking lot where you wanted to meet your
    children
so that you didn't mix your two families.
It sits there, a weathered, indestructible trunk
    that still comes between us, like love that
    becomes rusted and locked away.

Untitled
By Johnnierenee Nelson

We pass by Dora's burial box
wearing white yet once again
pretending to be sane

but that strip of brain tissue
which regulates most voluntary movements
flops like a freshly landed, oversized drum fish
behind our footsteps,

Now I think I know how Noah felt
having to mourn the deaths
of his grandfather, Methuselah
— his parents, his siblings

having survived the flood
only to debark from the ark
his whole world, a zoo.

Truckers' Tongue

By Kathleen Shumate

Our grand vacations when I was small,
St. Louis to San Diego,
a long haul down Route 66,
turn south at Flagstaff,
leave the Mother Road to her own course,
west at Gila Bend, and straight on till morning.

Out on the road, we'd speak the truckers'
      language:
flashing our brights from behind a semi,
who'd flash back at us once we were around.
Lights flicker thanks off and on at night
or on and off in the daylight.

Once in a while, we'd hoist our arms in the air
as we passed a shiny blue cab,
pull down pretending to ring a bell,
a horn would blast while we clapped
      and laughed.

Thirty-some years later,
I drive the route alone,
San Diego to Albuquerque,
still the truckers' trail
in spite of streamlined jets
and lickety-split railroad trains.

I tried to speak the truckers' language,
show I hadn't forgotten the polite signals;
only two answered and the rest didn't speak
even to each other for 840 light and dark miles,
a tongue now foreign to its native speakers.

Crestwood Summit

By Celia Sigmon

On the road, at seventy miles per hour,
  due East,
the sky was on fire, breaking blue as your eyes,
holding the empty space above me like a lover.
There at the top, with bursting sun I
  drove blind,
the sinking moon like a golden claw behind,
and skimmed the highway like skin to hear
  you speak,
to see your face. Content instead with lines
of water and fire, now words fill me when
  I hunger

and burn away the nights I lay ablaze,
scorched by a past recalled: a gentle bear,
both drawn and claimed by water, whose round
and cupping words still draw my breath
  from sleepless rest.
Who in one passing glance did turn that
  blue sky
that held me into a bright and lidless eye.

The Day's Peak
By Gabriela Anaya Valdepeña

With your entourage of dust devils,
you arrive at the day's peak.

The damaged day.
Damascus is lost. Mexico City —

maudlin clouds, dirty pillows,
oxygen tanks, cigarettes.

Women wrapped in flames.
I climb a pyramid.

At this height, nothing can hurt,
not even the fall.

You with your accent from
sleeping worlds. One shot.
I use all my words in one sentence.

You reject me for simplicity; brevity,
I can't say enough about this.

The last step. I
spread my arms like a charmed bird.
You are the first god, the third man,
the last animal.

What significance
does one number have over another —

a face,
a word?

122

Volunteers

"The fewer men, the greater share of honour. God's will! I pray thee, wish not one man more."
— from Shakespeare's *Henry V*

Chris Dickerson — the poet, university professor and pool shark — likes to joke that the volunteers who run Border Voices remind her of that unfortunate character played by Charlie Chaplin in the movie "Modern Times."

PLOT SUMMARY: Chaplin is put to work in a factory. An efficiency expert comes in and decides he can be more productive. The expert ties various tools to Chaplin's feet, neck, head — and then to other, less likely parts of the body. The frantic Chaplin is soon a whirling mechanical dervish . . .

Chris is right. Running a program like Border Voices using ONLY volunteers does have a Chaplinesque quality. Unpaid staffers write TV scripts during coffee breaks at their "real" jobs; they edit the annual anthologies late at night, when the kids (or the dogs) have gone to bed . . .

And some of us also find time to write poems.

This section of *The Best of Border Voices* contains some of those poems.

Not all the volunteers are represented here, of course. The president of San Diego State University — Stephen L. Weber — is on the Border Voices board and is great at hosting parties for people like Maya Angelou as well as providing general guidance — but he doesn't write much poetry. The same is true of other key volunteers.

But we have a good group of people and poets in this section anyway, including:

(1)   Longtime Border Voices fair manager **Chris Baron**, who also finds time to be a college professor. His moving poem "Dog Hill" resonates with courage and compassion, qualities that he exhibits daily in ways that bring joy to friends, co-workers and family.

(2)   **Chris Dickerson**, the editor of the annual anthologies. Chris says it was her involvement in Border Voices that led her to actually start WRITING poetry after many years of teaching it. She got an MFA in Creative Writing— but more importantly, she began writing poems whose language is sweet in the mouth, sensual and dense with imagery . . .

(3)   **Cathy Woo**, a member of the Border Voices board who also is an internationally known scholar, painter, poet, composer, and Feng Shui practitioner. She served on the National Council on the Arts from 1991 to 1996 — and she also found time to write poems that are playful, serious, and

touching (sometimes all three at the same time!) Many of her poems have been set to music — one of Asia's number one hit songs, "Day by Day by Day the Sky Is Blue," uses one of Cathy's poems for the lyrics.

(4) **Jack Webb**, founder-director of Border Voices — who, since he is writing this introduction, will let his poems speak for themselves.

(5) **Joan Webb**, another member of the board who offers an incredibly touching poem about her father . . .

And then there are the FORMER volunteers, whose selfless hard work will long be remembered: **M. Hope Meek**, **Sylvia Levinson**, **César A. González-T**. All three are good-hearted, talented people; a list of their accomplishments — in fields ranging from education and literature to computer management—would make a book all by itself.

Here are their poems, accomplishments of the heart and spirit written by people who took joy in nurturing the creativity of others, and found a little time to be creative themselves . . .

Dog Hill
By Chris Baron

I bend on the street corner,
relieved. The words of the Torah
spilling from my lips,
locked in practiced repetition.
am I a man?
the city's lost inside me
the bridges, Yankee Stadium,
I see the good in rain,
the truth in my father
like the uncertainty
of the first snow.
am I a man?
The edge of Dog Hill marks winter,
snow lines hide the drop of the hill,
a speedway of racing toboggans.
I pull my own "golden Eagle"
to the edge of the line, push off,
free-fall in biting wind.
    am I a man?
At the 96th street playground,
our eyes wide at the intricacies
of the metal slide complex,
impossible stairs entangled
in stairs, a cage in the center,
the mouth of the slide
impossible to reach.
And inside, Rebecca Mendel,
brown hair pulled tightly
in a ponytail — the thought
of her hair let down
had brought me here.
    am I a man?

At the museum my father
shows me our heritage.
Things never permitted,
once invisible, are now alive.
He shows me "Holocaust,"
fills in maps empty until now.
The photographs are pale black and white —
mothers in rags mix in iron crocks,
children gather at a street corner,
like tiny, full-grown men,
their hats pulled tight.
    will they be men?
They'll never read the book alone.
Families gather, light candles,
hold each other, walk together,
load on trucks, trains, wagons,
children smile, why wouldn't they,
This could be their greatest adventure.
    am I a man?
My father cups his hands around my face,
whispers, "never again." And I see for the first
      time
the fragile beauty of words,
of cities beneath cities, morning snow,
and returning home.

Intimations*
By Chris Dickerson

Do you hear the poplars, father,
droning and bending?
Their quiet rasp
brushes the twilight wash.

They too must know the stress
of capillaries starved
for bright red air; must fear
the brittle cold.

Your heart — one moment spun
in trembling waltz and in the next
too still — says, "Listen!" and we
strain to hear.

At any sudden gust the leaves
might shilly-shally, clack and rush
towards home. We watch them fall,
imagine that the last
kiss silence.

Popule Meus: Improperia Reproaches*
for CA Prop 187, 1994 / HR 4437, 2005
By César A. González-T.

"Patriotism is love for one's country, with the desire to make it better."
– San Diego Mesa College students, English 205

"Popule meus,
quid feci tibi,
aut in quo contristavi te?
Responde mihi."
"Oh, my people,
what have I done to you,
or in what have I offended you?
Answer me."

I sought work,
and you exploited my hunger.
I agreed to work for a pittance,
and you called the migra on payday.
I picked your fruits and your vegetables,
you poisoned me with pesticides,

I tended your gardens, your fields of flowers,
and you flogged me with thistles of sound bites.
I made your food, served you in
        your restaurants,
and you have heaped my plate with bile.
I sewed your clothes in your
        storefront sweatshops,
you threw me out naked into the night.
I watched over your children and loved them,
and you would terrorize even my
        unborn babies.

I cared for your incontinent and
      troubled old folks,
you turned my aged ones out to perish.
I cleaned your warm homes and filled them
      with love,
and you sent me into the pitiless night.
I have come whenever it suited you,
you have thrown me out when
      you were through with me;
you use my country as one would
      a whorehouse:
Take — without consequence or responsibility.

And now let me tell you what will
      happen to you:
God will curse you and divide you and
      you will be confounded.
You will attack others as you sing of
      "your country,"
and the world will condemn you.
The land that we would make great
will become the Divided States of
      North America;
you will be nobody's country
until you are everybody's country.

And so we pray:
Our Lady of Guadalupe, Patroness of
      the Americas,
Pray for us.
Frances Cabrini, North American saint and
      patroness of immigrants,
Pray for us.

And finally, with the prayer of the

United Nations, we ask for
unity among nations:
"Strike from our hearts
the national self-righteousness that causes
hatred and division
between persons and countries,"
we beseech thee, O Lord.
So be it.

Amen.

There's a Strange Light That Occurs[*]
By Sylvia Levinson

I look up from papers strewn on my desk
and the light is thick, orange-pink,
the house, dead-quiet,
day gone, night on the brink,
the world frozen in ephemeral silence —
before a phone rings, someone
        snaps the switch on a lamp.

The sun is setting into the Pacific
        a few miles away,
my view obscured by the building next door.
An olive tree outside my window holds
        residual light,

---

[*] Copyright © 2002 by Sylvia Levinson. Previously published in *Snowy Egret* (Spring 2003), and in the collection *Gateways: Poems of Nature, Meditation and Renewal* (Caernarvon Press, 2005). It also was included in the unpublished manuscript *Of the Body*, which won second-place honors at the San Diego Book Awards, 2003.

and some birds (I never know the names)
sing out the day, and the sky
which I can see above the rooftop,
is pewter-blue, its frayed hem fading into pink.

In this blessed part of my day, all is stillness,
only the low hum of my molecules audible,
and I hear my own cells singing.

Temple Bell[*]
By M. Hope Meek

a bronze bell hangs

from temple beams

hums in the wind

the grey log swings.

Vibrations of a thousand years.

---

[*] Copyright © by M. Hope Meek

A Bouquet for Her Birthday
By Jack Webb

I. First Poem for Her Birthday

Drapes blossom in sea wind, and now she sees
her children gather, and all those she loves,
smiling away the chill and sorrow that rub
the edges of each day: she is at peace,
and she dreams a little. It seems she holds
                    the key
to some great mystery, woven from the blooded
robes of martyred saints, or somehow grubbed
by a daughter's hand from earth, and tears,
                    and sweets.

She almost has it now, this frail thought –
that <u>we</u> are the gods we worship, those clouds
                    of glory
are for <u>us</u>, and our children, while our lives
                    are bought
by our own blood; we are the prophets, ours
                    the story . . .
but it's too late, and now she's glad.
                    Her children
turn away, voices drifting on the wind.

II. The Divine Pharmacy

This is the way to pray, as a child does,
in the morning, in a cloud of loves.
Fresh from confession, the wind dreaming
                    through him,
he imagines his soul is clean as milk;

the road is straight and smooth as silk
and edged with excitement. He veers,
praised by the cloudy eyes of seers,
and gaily waves to a forgotten self.

Let us learn, my love, to be child and
                mother both;
to see church and state and Hollywood
              as a boat
full of games most beautiful and rare,
pleasures which all history prepared
from what men dreamed of, and dared.
Then let us turn to one another,
find in our arms the child-mother,
and rest in the innocence beyond despair.

III. Little Poem

I owe you
a poem
that's honest
and true —
this paper,
these words
are the best
I can do.

I won't talk
of the moon
or walks
on the beach,
or how treasures
are found
each in each —

134

I'll give you
this poem,
so simple
and bold,
like love's first kiss
or the touch
of your lips.

While at Fisherman's Wharf in Monterey[*]
By Joan Webb

I spotted my favorite treat — a candy apple.
Oh, the red shiny sweet confection!
My father made candy apples every Halloween,
the smell of the candy cooking, the red drops
falling into the pot, the popsicle sticks
poised to pierce the apples, the smell
of burning leaves and the frosty pumpkins
glaring at us and at the center of everything
my father, with his candy apples.

---

[*] This poem was originally published in the October 2000 issue of *San Diego Writers' Monthly* under the name Joan Gardner.

Two Poems
By Dr. Catherine Yi-yu Cho Woo

1. Minute

In huge lake
   Floating
     On raft of
      Fallen leaf
Surrounded by
   Snow capped
     Peaks

Among nature's majestic view

   The part
  I'm playing
   So minute . . .

2. Don't Really Mind If I Never Wake

Bed of
  Pine needles

Quilt of
   Moonlight
     Heavenly tent of stars

Rapids
  Singing
    Lullaby
With loved one
    Only
     A thought away

Don't really mind
    If
   I never wake

136

Major Poets

THE KING'S CAMELEOPARD,
OR
THE ROYAL NONESUCH ! ! !

LADIES AND CHILDREN NOT ADMITTED.

"There," says the Duke, "if that line don't fetch them, I don't know Arkansaw!"
— from Mark Twain's
The Adventures of Huckleberry Finn

Strong you thump O terrible drums – so loud you bugles blow.
— Walt Whitman

If modern poetry didn't exist — with all its "alarums and excursions," its critical debates and opposing schools and savage broadsides — it would be hard to invent. It is, in fact, the strange and exotic blossom of a strange and exotic age, an age that was first espied from afar by the brilliant critic-poet-composer Ezra Pound, who lamented the fact that he lived in a time —

the early 20th Century — when the old philoso-
phies and religions were beginning to lose their
potency among intellectuals, artists and many
average citizens: "Ghosts move about me /
Patched with histories."

Pound saw the problem clearly: since
modern civilization is bereft of universal beliefs,
it is almost impossible to create a single unified
art form that will appeal to large numbers of
people. The epics, to take one example, were
beautifully designed to appeal to select and rela-
tively homogenous audiences: the citizens of
Rome and Athens, the city-states that ruled em-
pires.

The symbol of art in an age of fragmenta-
tion is NOT the epic: it is the TV remote control,
the electronic doorway to our divided attention .
. .

The problem seemed insoluble. But
Pound was a genius, and he thought he saw a
way forward for those who loved the old arts, es-
pecially poetry. His answer was to adopt multi-
ple and interchangeable voices to reflect the
multiple and equally valid viewpoints available
to a citizen of the modern world. His ambitious
and much-criticized attempt to turn this ap-
proach into art, in the "endless poem" he called
The Cantos, has inspired poets ever since.*

---

* Even before *The Cantos*, Pound was inspiring his con-
temporaries with his novel theories. The young T.S. Eliot
came under his wing and used Pound' s flawless ear-for-
sound to help him edit *The Wasteland* – the great poem of
Modernism that Eliot originally wanted to call (in a nod
perhaps to Pound's theories of multiple personae) "He Do
the Police in Many Voices."

In the next few pages, you will get a close-up look at the impact of Pound's brilliant theories, personality and poetic example on today's artists. That close-up look will focus on 29 poets, all of whom appeared at various Border Voices poetry fairs since 1994. You will see them play with language in ways that are both fun and instructive: you will hear the thump of "terrible drums . . . (the) bugles blow . . ." You will catch the echoes of debate as critics lose sight of Pound's great example, and — adrift in a sea of perplexity — cling desperately to various fixed ideas about art.

Right this way, folks. The stage is set, the lights are dim, and the King's Cameleopard — the Royal Nonesuch — is about to make his historic-and-long-awaited entrance at last . . .

Francisco X. Alarcón*

2003 Border Voices Poetry Fair

Francisco X. Alarcón, Chicano poet and educator, was born in 1954 and lived the first six years of his life in Wilmington, CA. As a child, he also lived in Guadalajara, Mexico, but he has been living in California since he was 18. He is the author of 10 volumes of poetry, including, *From the Other Side of Night / Del otro lado de la noche: New and Selected Poems* (University of Arizona Press 2002), *Sonetos a la locura y otras penas / Sonnets to Madness and Other Misfortunes* (Creative Arts Book Company 2001), *No Golden Gate for Us* (Pennywhistle Press 1993), *Snake Poems: An Aztec Invocation* (Chronicle Books 1992), *De amor oscuro / Of Dark Love* (Moving Parts Press 1991, and 2001), *Body in Flames / Cuerpo en llamas* (Chronicle Books 1990).

---

* Photo by Francisco Dominguez.

His most recent book of bilingual poetry for children is *Poems to Dream Together / Poemas para soñar juntos* (Lee & Low Books 2005). A previous bilingual book for children, *Laughing Tomatoes and Other Spring Poems / Jitomates risueños y otros poemas de primavera* (Children's Book Press, 1997) was awarded the 1997 Pura Belpré Honor Award by the American Library Association and the National Parenting Publication's Gold Medal. He also received the 2000 Pura Belpré Honor Award for his second book of bilingual poems for children, *From the Bellybutton of the Moon and Other Summer Poems / Del ombligo de la luna y otros poemas de verano* (Children's Book Press 1998), and the 2002 Pura Belpré Honor Award for another book of bilingual poems for children, *Iguanas in the Snow and Other Winter Poems / Iguanas en la nieve y otros poemas de invierno* (Children's Book Press 2001). He has published one other book for children, *Angels Ride Bikes and Other Fall Poems / Los ángeles andan en bicicleta y otros poemas de otoño* (Children's Book Press 1999).

Alarcón currently teaches at the University of California, Davis, where he directs the Spanish for Native Speakers Program.

Francisco X. Alarcón, poeta y educador chicano, nació en 1954 y pasó los primeros seis años de su vida en Wilmington, California. De niño vivió en Guadalajara, México, pero desde los dieciocho años ha residido en el estado de California en EE.UU. Es el autor de diez volúmenes de poesía que incluyen: *From the Other Side of Night*

/ *Del otro lado de la noche: New and Selected Poems* (University of Arizona Press 2002), *No Golden Gate for Us* (Pennywhistle Press 1993), *Sonetos a la locura y otras penas / Sonnets to Madness and Other Misfortunes* (Creative Arts Book Company 2001), *Snake Poems: An Aztec Invocation* (Chronicle Books 1992), *De amor oscuro / Of Dark Love* (Moving Parts Press, 2001), *Cuerpo en llamas / Body in Flames* (Chronicle Books 1990).

Su libro más reciente de poesía bilingüe para niños es *Poems to Dream Together / Poemas para soñar juntos* (Lee & Low Books 2005). Su previo libro de poemas bilingües para niños titulado *Jitomates risueños y otros poemas de primavera* (Children's Book Press 1997) fue galardoneado con el premio 1997 Pura Belpré Honor Award otorgado por la American Library Association. Tambien recibió el premio 2000 Pura Belpré Honor Award por su segundo libro de poemas bilingües para niños, *Del ombligo de la luna y otros poemas de verano* (Children's Book Press 1998), y el premio 2002 Pura Belpré Honor Award por su libro de poemas bilingües para niños, *Iguanas en la nieve y otros poemas de invierno* (Children's Book Press 2001). Ha publicado otro libro para niños titulado *Los ángeles andan en bicicleta y otros poemas de otoño* (Children's Book Press 1999).

Actualmente enseña en el Depamento de Español de la Universidad de California en Davis donde es Director del Programa de Español para Hispanohablantes.

Sabrosa bendición*

para una noche
oscura y fría
este dulce calor
que da alegría

cuando se siente
mucha soledad
este tranquilizante
sonido del hogar:

choco
> *choco*
>> *bate*
>>> *bate*

es mi abuelita
dispuesta a sacar
con su molinillo
espuma sin parar:

choco
> *choco*
>> *bate*
>>> *bate*

¡qué sabroso
el chocolate
que mi abuelita
recalienta y bate!

---

* Copyright © 2006 by Francisco X. Alarcón. From a new, unpublished collection of bilingual poems titled "Day Poems." Printed here by permission of the author.

Delicious Blessing

for a cold
moonless night
this warm
sweet delight

when feeling
all alone
this soothing
sound of home:

chock
   chock
      beat
         beat

it's Grandma
working a foam
by keep making
her beater moan:

chock
   chock
      beat
         beat

her chocolate
in the heat
more delicious
with each beat!

My Kind of Day[*]

Saturday is
really by far
my kind of day

no school today!
I feel free like
a hummingbird!

I can go to the park
team up with friends
and play soccer

or help my sister
assemble a kite
and make it fly

on Saturday
the blue of the sky
is even bluer

Mi día favorito

el sábado es
de todos de veras
mi día favorito

---

[*] Copyright © 2006 by Francisco X. Alarcón. From a new, unpublished collection of bilingual poems titled "Day Poems." Printed here by permission of the author.

145

¡no hay escuela hoy!
¡y yo me siento libre
como un colibrí!

al parque puedo ir
y con mis amigos
jugar fútbol

o ayudar a mi hermana
a armar un papalote
y hacerlo volar

el sábado
el azul del cielo
es hasta más azul

Cuatro estaciones
en un día[*]

en el sur
de California
un día puede tener

las cuatro
estaciones
del año

la primavera
llega muy

---

de mañana

el verano
va a la playa
al mediodía

el otoño sale
como niebla
al atardecer

el invierno vuelve
a las montañas
al anochecer

*Four Seasons
in One Day*

in Southern
California
a day could have

the four
seasons
of the year

spring
arrives early
with the morning

at noon
summer goes
to the beach

after dusk

a sea fog rolls
cool as fall

winter goes to
the mountains
back for the night

David Antin
2003 Border Voices Poetry Fair

Poet, performance art-
ist and literary critic
David Antin is interna-
tionally known for his
"talk pieces"— im-
provisational blends of
comedy, story and so-
cial commentary that
critics have described
as "a cross between
Lenny Bruce and
Ludwig Wittgenstein"
or (alternately) as "a
blend of Mark Twain
and Gertrude Stein."
New Directions has
published three books
of Antin's "talk pieces": *Talking at the Bounda-
ries* (1976), *Tuning* (1984), and *What It Means to
be Avant-Garde* (1993). *Tuning* was awarded the
prize for poetry for 1984 by the PEN Center of
Los Angeles.

Antin, who has performed at venues ranging
from the Whitney Museum and the Guggenheim
to the Musée d'Art Moderne in Paris, has also
designed Skypoems — short texts which he de-

scribes as "commercials that aren't selling any-thing"– that have been sky-typed over Los Ange-les and San Diego. He also designed "Word Walks" for urban parks as well as an ongoing electronic poem for an airport, and he has per-formed both improvised and scripted verbal works for radio and television.

His brilliant and often-humorous improvisa-tions have captured the attention of critics, in-cluding Marjorie Perloff, who wrote about him in *The Poetics of Indeterminacy* (Princeton, 1981). More recently, he was featured in Charles O. Hartman's *The Jazz Text* (Princeton, 1991), while the "Review of Contemporary Fiction" devoted its entire Spring 2001 issue to his work.

In 2001 Granary Books published *A Conver-sation with David Antin*, the text of a three-month e-mail conversation between Antin and Charles Bernstein. More recent works include a new collection of talk pieces: *i never knew what time it was* (University of California Press, 2005), which one reviewer described as "richly funny, elegiac, philosophical, contentious, filled with astonishing stories and bizarre characters." Also published in 2005: *john cage uncaged is still cagey* (Singing Horse Press). The latter book, Antin says, "originated from two performance (talk) pieces I did for John at the Strathmore Festival celebrating his 77th birthday in 1989. He was present at both talks." Cage, of course, was the composer-visual artist-poet — and Zen Buddhist / mushroom collector!! — who (like Antin) was famous for his non-traditional ap-proach to the making of art.

Antin is professor emeritus of visual arts at the University of California, San Diego.

regarding a door[*]

regarding a door
its open and shut
but it is less open and shut than a wall
a wall is something to lean on
but its unwise to lean on a door
regarding a door
you can take it in hand
turning the knob of a door you can open it and
        step through
then its no longer a door
now in the case of a wall
its a wall wherever you are
which is evident and consoling
with a wall you always know where you are
while a door is only a door from outside
there is also something substantial about walls
maybe its the material from which theyre made
the bricks and the plaster
more likely its the absence of hinges
the hinges in doors are like hidden conditions
upon which everything turns
theyre like the small print in contracts
a door depends on its hinges
but it also depends on a wall

theres nothing unusual about a wall without

---

     doors
a door without a wall is ridiculous
also a door is usually visible in all of its limits
but you cannot see the other side of a wall
and a door is always suggesting another side
so doors seem ambiguous and appear to be for-
ever flapping
      in the wind
a revolving door seems to be always changing
         its mind
but regarded from whatever angle
it is always offering you the same proposition
there are many unanswered questions
      about doors
why is it that there arent circular or
       elliptical doors
what is it thats frightening about sliding doors
and what about the colors of doors
green doors in brick walls
white doors in black walls
or black doors in any walls
this will lead you to suspect that im talking
      about symbols
rather than about doors and walls
whats all this talk about doors and
      walls anyway
why not talk about something real
like strainers

Alberto Blanco*
1999 Border Voices Poetry Fair

I try my BEST to be just like I AM ...
but everybody WANTS you to be just like THEM ...
they say "sing while you SLAVE" ...
I just get BORED ...
I AIN'T gonna work on Maggie's FARM no more ...
— Bob Dylan: from his song "Maggie's Farm"

Alberto Blanco is SUCH a sweet guy. Forget the fact that he can talk with authority about chemical va-  lences, ancient Aztec art or the boy-Einstein's hatred of formal schooling . . . and do it fluently in Spanish OR English. Forget that Blanco is a chemist-poet- philosopher-rock musician- scholar . . . a true polymath who has been called one of Latin America's greatest writers ... but who cares? The important thing is the exemplary and instructive sensibility that shines through his poetry, as in the exquisite "Horse by Moonlight" that accompanies this short bio, or the following short masterpiece,

---

* Photo by Linda Lasky

translated by Robert L. Jones (and edited down to a few key lines so it can be wedged into this brief exegesis):

THE POET DOES AND DOES NOT HAVE

He doesn't have the poverty of Christ
He doesn't have the speed of zen ...

He does have the solemnity of a fifteen-year-old
He does have the sense of humor of a tractor

This is simple and endearing stuff, right? Nothing like what you would expect if you believed what some critics say about Blanco, as (for example) in this baffling little piece:

> (Blanco's) style is unmistakably his own, with his constant word play (and) its fearless appropriation of the quotidian . . . a feverish mist of words.

(TIP FOR YOUNG WRITERS: You can generally tell a critic doesn't know what he's talking about when he uses a lot of big words where little ones will do — for example "quotidian" instead of "every day" — and then starts rushing along breathlessly mumbling about "mists of words." Shun such critics as you would a poison toad: they do NOT mean you well).

In a TV interview with Border Voices, Blanco explored the whole question of art and education in the 21st Century, and incidentally provided a helpful key to much of his own poetry. Here are a few excerpts:

ON EDUCATION, ART & REBELLION: "Children understand that deep feeling of not wanting to be other than what they are . . . But everything around them tells them they need to be better or stronger or more beautiful than they are . . . Traditional schools are still doing a very good job of frustrating kids that way . . ."

"I knew from an early age that things were not the way my parents and teachers said . . . but as a kid, it's hard to gather enough energy to make it clear to others around you that what they say is not quite so . . . I was 16 or 18 when I first said it out loud . . . and naturally it caused a lot of problems, with my father, my teachers . . . they said 'all you have to do is follow instructions.'"

"The kids can feel when there's an open space where they can breathe. But parents and teachers must provide that open space in the most sincere way . . . the teacher can do it by displaying his own creativity right there in the classroom."

WHY HE'S WRITTEN SO MANY ANIMAL POEMS: "I've written so much about animals because I miss them so much . . . the way we live now, in the cities, we are far away from the wild world . . . I feel this deep longing . . . we have animals not only outside, in the wilds or the zoo, but also inside . . . in our dreams, and from a biological point of view, they are here, in our vertebrae . . . they are a part of the tribe."

Blanco has published 25 books of poetry as well as art essays, poetry translations and selections for children. His books of poetry include *Cromos* (1987), which won the Carlos Pellicer poetry award, and *Canto a la sombra de los animales* (1988), which won the José Fuentes Mares national prize. A bilingual anthology of his poems, *Dawn of the Senses*, was published in 1996 by City Lights Books.

As of this writing, Blanco had just been appointed "Knapp Chair" at the University of San Diego. The position of Knapp Chair brings distinguished visiting scholars to the USD campus.

Caballo A La Luz De La Luna[*]

Un caballo se escapó — del circo
y se internó — en los ojos de mi hija:
all se puso a dar vueltas alrededor del iris
levantando una polvareda plateada en la pupila
y deteniéndose de vez en cuando
a beber el agua santa de la retina.

Desde entonces mi hija siente un anhelo
de llanuras de pasto y colinas verdes . . .
as pasa largas horas en la ventana
esperando a que llegue la luna
a secar con sus mangas de seda
el agua triste que moja sus mejillas.

---

* Reprinted by permission of the author. This poem appeared in the book *Dawn of the Senses*, © 1995 City Lights Books. The English translation is by Jennifer Clement.

Horse by Moonlight

A horse escaped from the circus
and lodged in my daughter's eyes:
there he ran circles around the iris
raising silver dust-clouds in the pupil
and halting sometimes
to drink from the holy water of the retina.

Since then my daughter feels a longing
for meadows of grass and green hills . . .
she spends long hours at the window
waiting for the moon to come
and dry with its silk sleeves
the sad water that wets her cheeks.

Eavan Boland[*]

1999 Border Voices Poetry Fair

"Eavan Boland is the real thing."
— **James Merrill**

Like her divided land, Irish writer Eavan Boland's poetry is full of apparent contradictions. A list of those contradictions would include: 1. her championing of feminism and her reservations about its place in poetry ("Separatist ideology . . . pleads with the woman poet to discard the complexities of true feeling for the relative simplicity of anger"); 2. her heroic attempt to write about those she believes are "outside history" or outside the poetic tradition — especially poor women — and her competing sense that those lives, which she writes about with fondness, can nevertheless be most aptly described as "the silent and the futile and the absurd and the pointless."

It is Boland's attempt to rewrite that futility, to find a way out through a revisioning of women's historic roles, that — however full of

---

[*] Photo by Sara Barrett

acknowledged inconsistencies — has created a large place for her in the modern poetic canon.

Eavan Boland was born in 1944, the daughter of diplomat Frederick H. Boland and artist Frances Kelly. She spent her childhood in London — "a city of fogs and strange consonants" — where her father served as ambassador to London, and returned to Ireland as a teenager to attend Trinity College and write poetry.

The crisis came in the late '60s, when — as an instructor at Trinity College — she found herself confronted with two dilemmas: first, "I didn't have the ability or the taste" to be an academic, and, second, her growing sense that "the map of Irish poetry, which for ages has been drawn by men, was one on which I did not find my name written." Quitting Trinity, Boland began what in retrospect can be seen as a 20-year exile that was also an intense poetic exploration. She built a relatively insular life with her husband, the novelist Kevin Casey, and her two daughters; at the same time she sought to find a new language and subject matter for her poetry, one in which there was "no contradiction between the way I lifted a child or made an assonance." Recognition of her achievement grew slowly, and awards and honors followed.

Eavan Boland has published eight volumes of poetry, the most recent being *In a Time of Violence* and *An Origin Like Water: Collected Poems 1967-87*, both with W.W. Norton. Her most recent published book is *Against Love Poetry* (2001). She has received the Lannan Award for Poetry and has published a volume of prose called *Object Lessons: The Life of the Woman and the Poet in Our Time.*

She is currently head of the creative writing department at Stanford University.

The Blossom*

A May morning.
Light starting in the sky.
I have come here
after a long night.
Its senses of loss.
Its unrelenting memories of happiness.

The blossom on the apple tree is still in shadow,
its petals half-white and filled with water at the
core,
in which the freshness and secrecy of dawn are
stored
even in the dark.

How much longer
will I see girlhood in my daughter?

In other seasons
I knew every leaf on this tree.
Now I stand here
almost without seeing them

and so lost in grief

---

* Reprinted by permission of the author. This poem was first published in *The New Yorker.*

I hardly notice what is happening
as the light increases and the blossom speaks,
and turns to me
with blonde hair and my eyebrows and says —

imagine if I stayed here,
even for the sake of your love,
what would happen to the summer?
To the fruit?

Then holds out a dawn-soaked hand to me,
whose fingers I counted at birth
years ago.

And touches mine for the last time.

And falls to earth.

Marilyn Chin*
1994 & 2002 Border Voices Poetry fairs

BARE-BONES BIO: Born in Hong Kong in 1955, poet Marilyn Chin was brought to the United States soon after. One of her father's first decisions as a newly minted American citizen was to change his daughter's name from Mei Ling to Marilyn, in honor of the blonde bombshell movie star with whom he was obsessed. While Chin says she now accepts the name and no longer seeks to change it, she remains an activist poet who sees herself pitted against the dominant culture in which she lives. Her lyrical and delicately metered verse enchants the ear while challenging assumptions, and she has won many awards for her poetry including four Pushcart Prizes. She was featured on Bill Moyers' PBS series "The Language of Life," and currently co-directs the Master of Fine Arts Program in Creative Writing at San Diego State University. She has published three collections of poetry: *Dwarf Bamboo*; *The Phoenix Gone, The Terrace Empty*; and *Rhapsody in Plain Yellow*.

* Photo by Niki Berg

TIPS FOR YOUNG WRITERS: Reading Marilyn Chin is to descend into phantasmorgia, as images and attitudes from ancient China impinge on the present. As in the accompanying poem, the reader is frequently unsure whether the poem is set in the 21st century or the Ming dynasty, whether the sobbing mother in another poem is preparing turtle soup from a can, or from the carcass of an animal that washed up on some pebbled Asian beach in 1398 A.D. Often, the answer seems to be that both things are occurring at the same time, as part of a trope or extended metaphor that conveys Chin's protest against modern-day colonialism. The trope is marvelously effective, giving her work the sting of exile. We become increasingly aware and sympathetic to the fact that Chin is exiled from her motherland, from a way of life and language, and as we read on, we begin to participate in that exile.

Chin's haunting style — the specific technique she uses to shape her words — shares the paradoxes of her world vision: it is a style that is both Chinese and English, in very precise and provocative ways.

The characteristic Chin style can be seen as directly influenced by the early-20th century experimentalists (e.g. Ezra Pound), who developed the methodology of *flatness* — of piling one concrete statement on top of another until the images generate an emotion by themselves. Pound and other so-called "moderns" came up with the idea of *flatness* by themselves, but evolution of the method was accelerated by the discovery and translation of ancient Chinese poems that had already exploited the technique with extraordinary effectiveness. Thus, Chin's work can be seen — even in the texture of its language — to be both a tribute and implicit criticism of two cultures.

Unrequited Love*

Because you stared into the black lakes of her eyes,
you shall drown in them.

Because you tasted the persimmon on her lips,
you shall dig your moist grave.

Her rope of black hair does not signify a ladder of
    escape,
but of capture,

the warm flesh of her arms and thighs — not
    cradles of comfort,
but of despair.

She shall always be waiting for you in an empty room

---

overlooking the sea.

She shall always sit this way, her back toward you,
her shoulders bare,

her silk kimino in manifolds around her waist —
blue as the changeless sea.

You sit prostrate before her, bruise your fore-
head,
chant the Dharmas.

Five thousand years together in the same
    four-and-a-mat room,
and she has not learned to love you.

Billy Collins*

2000 & 2002 Border Voices Poetry fairs

BARE-BONES BIO: Billy Collins surprised a substantial segment of America's self-proclaimed literary elite when he was named U.S. poet laureate in 2001. His witty verse seemed far too fun-loving to be worthy of the highest honors. Even worse, he had managed to capture a huge readership in an age when poetry's audience has dwindled. For the lemon-lipped *literati* ensconced in tiny subsidized magazines, Collins' string of poetic best-sellers seemed unpleasantly non-bohemian: there was the whiff of capitalism about it. But Collins managed to handle his notoriety — as well as a punishing schedule of readings and other public service — with only occasional lapses in his usual wry humor. Through it all, as poet-critic Edward Hirsch noted, Collins remained "an American original — a metaphysical poet with a funny bone and a sly questioning intelligence."

---

* Photo by Jersey Walz

Collins is a Distinguished Professor of English at Lehman College, City University of New York. He has published eight collections of poetry including *Questions About Angels* (1991); *The Art of Drowning* (1995); *Picnic, Lightning* (1998); *Nine Horses* (2002); *Sailing Alone Around the Room: New and Selected Poems* (2001); and *The Trouble with Poetry* (2005).

TIPS FOR YOUNG WRITERS: When a contemporary poet is an artistic and financial success, it can be difficult to determine the reasons for it, and to learn from his methods. All the hoopla surrounding the poet tends to obscure his or her real achievements.

Collins's success can be traced in part to his training as a professor of Romantic poetry. He has adopted the techniques of the great 18th and 19th Century poets he studies as an academic: he writes poems that are personal, emotional, agreeable and reflective, something like Wordsworth's "Tintern Abbey" but with humor. Like the late e. e. cummings, Collins has obtained celebrity by offering readers what they have been famished for — poems that are easy to read and melodious to the ear, and in that way totally unlike the deliberately "anti-popular" verse of many latter-day poets; but at the same time, Collins' poems — like those of cummings — wear an intriguing mask of modernity because of their hip quirkiness.

The young writer also cannot ignore how Collins so easily moves from the whimsical to darker emotions, and back again — as in "My Heart," in which he observes that his heart may once have been fit for "long-forgotten rituals, perhaps / of a sacrificial nature."

Long practice has made Collins capable of spurts of creativity at a very high level. I once joined Collins at an event in Sacramento, at which — in front of a crowd of 1,000 educators — he read a poem he'd written as his plane was landing. The poem was hilarious, richly textured, solid as an old coin, shining as if fresh from the mint — as indeed it was.

Yellow Berries*

I stop to look into the undergrowth
at the edge of a green playing field —
a tangle of bushes,
small yellow berries in clusters.

No scalpel is singing
across my abdomen this morning,

nor have I been tied to a chair
in order to be questioned, slapped,
and questioned again.

And this gives me the time
to stand here and wonder
whether these berries are safe to eat or not
if I were starving, say,

---

* Copyright © 1999 by Billy Collins. This charming poem was printed, for the first time anywhere, in the seventh annual Border Voices anthology in 2000. It is reprinted here with the permission of the author.

if there were no nearby market
where all kinds of berries
may be purchased in great quantities.

Three sparrows,
who probably know the answer,
surprise me when they twitter up from the knot-
ted   vines
and as I watch them fly off,

I decide that when the day comes,
I will refuse to die,
just chin-up-arms-folded refuse,
unless I am guaranteed clusters
of yellow berries
hanging in the afterlife,

a spacious green field,
and learned birds darting through the air.

My Heart[*]

It has a bronze covering inlaid with silver,
originally gilt;
the sides are decorated with openwork
        zoomorphic
panels depicting events in the history
of an unknown religion.

The convoluted top-piece shows a high
level of relief articulation
as do the interlocked spirals at the edges.

It was presumably carried in the house-shaped
reliquary alongside it, an object of exceptional
ornament, one of the few such pieces extant.
The handle, worn smooth, indicates its use
in long-forgotten rituals, perhaps
of a sacrificial nature.

It is engirdled with an inventive example
of gold interlacing, no doubt of Celtic influence.
Previously thought to be a pre-Carolingian
       work,
it is now considered to be of more
       recent provenance,
probably the early 1940s.

The ball at the center, visible
through the interstices of the lead webbing
and the elaborate copper grillwork,
is composed possibly of jelly
or an early version of water,
certainly a liquid, remarkably suspended
within the intricate craftsmanship
       of its encasement.

Jayne Cortez

2001 Border Voices Poetry Fair

Poet-playwright David Mills has written that Jayne Cortez's work is "about revolution and rhythm marinated in surrealism . . . an assault with a deadly and exotic feather: a seer's pen." All true enough at times, but I would add that it is also a lot of fun — especially on her CD's, where her brassy and frequently humorous lyrics are beautifully complemented by her elegantly complex, earthy voice and the deft riffs of various jazz musicians.

One of my favorite cuts is the title song on her 1996 CD, "Taking the Blues Back Home," in which Cortez laments that huge corporations now use the blues — the songs of the early, painful African experience in America —to sell their products. She then boldly states that

I'm taking the blues back home
I'm taking the blues back home . . .
I'm taking the blues back to where
The blues stealers won't go
I'm taking the blues back home before
Langston Hughes returns to say

171

"They're taking my blues again and gone"
I'm taking the blues back home . . .
I'm the owner of the blues
& I'm taking the blues back home

Poems like those on the accompanying page
lose something without her voice and/or music
behind them: as you read it, you might imagine
yourself in a dimly lit cabaret, the ghost of extin-
guished cigarettes in the air. There's the low
moan of a sax, then a rare and lovely voice:
"Yesterday took off its shoes . . . "

A BRIEF BIOGRAPHY: Jayne Cortez was born
in Arizona, grew up in California, and currently
lives in New York City. She is the author of 10
books of poetry and has performed her poetry
with music on nine recordings or CDs. She has
presented her works and ideas around the
world, from the Museum of Modern Art in New
York to the Fourth World Congress on Women in
Beijing and the Banlieues Bleues Festival in
France.

Cortez's numerous honors include an Ameri-
can Book Award and the International African
Festival Award, as well as a National Endow-
ment for the Arts fellowship. Her work as an ac-
tivist and organizer includes the presidency of
the Organization of Women Writers of Africa and
coordination of the Yari Yari Conference of
Women Writers of African Descent. Her most
recent books are *Jazz Fan Looks Back* (Hanging
Loose Press, 2002) and *Somewhere in Advance
of Nowhere* (Serpent's Tail/High Risk Books,
1996).

The Mambo Lesson*

Yesterday took off its shoes
and became an unpopular song
today will end like a stunned fish in
tomorrow's unequal distribution of
emptiness
as the sun makes its entrance
without public support into
the clairvoyance of your
unsweetened panty hose
& I am already
smoking an image
that will bite me
before I change my tongue
so don't forget your skull
your fossil fuel
your utopian teeth

---

* Copyright © 2006 by Jayne Cortez

Robert Creeley*

2004 Border Voices Poetry Fair

Not everybody loved Robert Creeley OR his poetry . . . as he cheerfully explained to two students on a Border Voices TV show back in 2004.

The way Creeley talked about "those who did not love him" — and the affectionate way the students interacted with Creeley — tell the careful reader a LOT about how a great artist wins friends and collaborators, as Creeley did again and again throughout his long and illustrious career.

"I remember Ezra Pound saying that you have to learn to take your wounds gladly," Creeley told the students. "It's not easy. For example, the first time I ever received recognition was in the *New York Times* . . . that was certainly the big time . . . and the critic said 'there are two things to be said about Robert Creeley's poems — They are short; they are not short enough.' "

---

* Photo by Michael Romanos.

"Ouch!" said one student. "How awful!!" said the other. Creeley just grinned.

"After the first expectable waves of anger, you learn not to pay attention," Creeley said. "By the time you DO win acceptance, you generally don't need it, and you learn that it's basically one's company, the people one lives with, that are important . . ."

"Friendship," said one of the students — an 11-year-old girl — in a tiny warm voice.

"Yes, friendship is the absolute basis," Creeley said, rewarding the girl with a note of awed respect in his voice, as if she had said something absolutely brilliant — as indeed she had.

A NOTE FROM THE EDITOR: Robert Creeley died on March 20, 2005. A little more than a month later, he was buried in Mount Auburn, America's first garden cemetery where Longfellow, Oliver Wendell Holmes, and other greats are also buried. The garden was in full bloom, grey misty shades of green, white, and pink, and Lawrence Ferlinghetti was later to capture that moment in the great elegy he wrote during the April 29 Border Voices poetry fair.

That elegy is printed here. I remember Ferlinghetti working on it beside the pool in my backyard, fretting that he wasn't getting it right, that he wasn't really capturing his love for his great friend.

He got it right.

He also proved once again that Creeley had good judgment both in selecting his friends and in making career choices, even when those choices, at the time, seemed reckless to casual observers.

Besides his brilliant poetry, Creeley is famous for dropping out of Harvard just before getting his degree. Instead, he starting writing letters to noted poets, soliciting poems for a magazine he was going to publish but never did. But he made a LOT of friends in the process, including Charles Olson, the ground-breaking experimental writer who got Creeley a key teaching and magazine-editing job at Black Mountain College. This successful friendship turned out to be the start of a career that generated more than 60 books of poetry and numerous awards, including the Lannan Lifetime Achievement Award.

Creeley was also remarkable for collaborating with jazz musicians, painters and composers, probably more than any other poet in the last 50 years.

This gift for friendship and collaboration would have been useless without his great talent for words, however, a talent so unusual that it created a whole army of admirers and imitators. "If you read too much Creeley," said poet William Corbett, "which I of course did, then you started writing like him with short perfect lines, simple nouns and verbs, short little ditties that were oblique and tantalizing with innuendo. Opening up any poetry magazine of the time you could find young poets scattered across the United States who had been snorting and smoking too much Creeley."

As many still do. He's that good.

At Creeley's Grave[*]

In the Creeley family plot in Mount Auburn Cemetery, Boston, just off the Tulip Path, there were already thirteen Creeleys and seven related Lauries with their names incised in a twelve-foot stone pillar, and poet Robert Creeley himself now just buried here still awaiting a gravestone under a Douglas Fir and a European Beech whose blossoms this windy wet April wave in the wrought air above him, and there they are, these "swamp Yankees" (as those were called who arrived too late or too poor to get hillside land) and here they all are now assembled with their new arrival, poet Creeley with his one eye (with which he saw more than any of us — and not just "what's passing by the window") and even that one wild wide eye blinded now, and the lidded sun dripping a drear tear as a light rain comes on, with a single big bird flying about from tree to tree, perfectly silent, and the poet's ancestors here assembled all perfectly silent and sightless too with their new companion lost in eternity — dear poet, dear brother, dear son!

— **Lawrence Ferlinghetti**

---

[*] Copyright © by Lawrence Ferlinghetti

Sad Advice*

If it isn't fun, don't do it.
You'll have to do enough that isn't.

Such is life, like they say,
no one gets away without paying

and since you don't get to keep it
anyhow, who needs it.
     — Robert Creeley

---

* "Sad Advice" from *ON EARTH* by Robert Creeley, © 2006 Estate of Robert Creeley. Published by University of California Press. Reprinted with the permission of the publisher and the support of Penelope Creeley.

178

Glover Davis*
1996 Border Voices Poetry Fair

BARE-BONES BIO: Glover Davis' poetry has been described as "powerful, magical, transforming" by a reviewer for the Wesleyan University Press. Former director of the Master of Fine Arts Program in Creative Writing at San Diego State University, Davis has published  four books of poetry, including *Bandaging Bread* (1971), *August Fires* (1978), and *Separate Lives* (Pecan Grove Press, 2006). The accompanying poem is from *Legend* (Wesleyan University Press, 1988).

A PERSONAL NOTE FROM THE EDITOR: Glover Davis, a bearish man with bristly blond hair so white it almost glows, was my first honest-to-goodness poetry professor. Like many another poet wannabe, I tended to hero-worship the great historic writers of verse, and Glover understood that genuflection of the soul — he, too, had a deep affection for Yeats, for Shakespeare, and for the lean tough poetry of Philip Levine, a Fresno poet who — many years before

---

* Photo by Sandy Davis.

— had shepherded Glover in his initial steps through the minefields of literary academe.

But Glover also had a touch of the jock about him. Glover (the name rhymes with "glove," rather than "clover") liked to reminisce about his days as a college student, his rare victories on the football field ("after two seasons of getting beat up on the scrimmage line, I knew I had to be a poet"), and the wild adventures of his fellow students, who loved midnight rides on motorcycles through the hills of Northern California as much as they loved reciting poetry.

"All poets are crazy," Glover would say in his more morose moments. "They have to be to devote themselves to a craft that pays so little." In his happier moments, however, Glover would confess that it was the mystery and magic — the sheer power — of poetry that had drawn him to it.

"If Levine hadn't been a poet, he would have been dictator of the world," Glover said. "He knew the power of rhythm to move us. He could have been the greatest demagogue ever."

Glover taught at SDSU for 39 years, retired, and moved back to Fresno, where he'd received his B.A.

Fresno has a vibrant poetry community, and Glover loves being there with old friends. But maybe he can feel a trembling underfoot, as the whole state shifts under the powerful weight of San Diego's disappointment at his departure.

Beneath Venetian Blinds*

When the angel spoke through lattices of flame
you napped, lethargic in the summer heat
and what those fluttering bands of light might
claim
from you, you would not see as beat by beat
wings hammered into blue and disappeared.
You thought it was only the wind in blinds.
You thought the panes where two worlds might
have   sheared —
light stippled, moist — where imagination as-
signs
to pure intelligence an aureole
of blood or whatever else the heart may need
could be ignored, and it was easy, dull
and torpid as you were till bead by bead
the drumming sprinkler made the colors run.
A darkening room impelled you toward the glass.
Your cheek a hot house petal, pressed and dun,
stuck with your breath and hair in a morass
of bluish green, a knuckle might have smashed.
Beyond all this there was a garden laved
with air and trellises where the wind slashed
branches swept up a light, red buds engraved.
But you had missed the import when you ig-
nored
gardens for syllables that spelt distress.
Thinking that this is what the flaming sword
of Eden is, you rose at dusk and dressed.

---

* Copyright © Glover Davis. From *Legend* (Wesleyan University Press, 1988). Reprinted with the permission of the author.

Lawrence Ferlinghetti

1997 and 2005 Border Voices Poetry fairs

Lawrence Ferlinghetti is a legend — but for back-stage workers at the fourth annual Border Voices fair, the most memor-able thing about him was a teen's enthu-siastic kiss, planted right in the middle of his bald-ing head.

That kiss had been completely unexpected just minutes before, when Ferlinghetti, after reading poetry to an enthusiastic crowd of 1,100, retreated to the dressing room.

As Ferlinghetti settled down, Border Voices directors heard a ruckus from the main hall; they ran out to find ushers wrestling with a mob of teens.

"I didn't think 78-year-old poets had group-ies!" one usher said.

"It looks like Ferlinghetti does," I said.

One young girl looked especially forlorn, beret slipping off her blonde curls, buds of tears in her eyes. "I HAVE to see Mr. Ferlinghetti," she said. "I have something to give him" . . . As she spoke, her fingers uncurled to reveal a brightly polished stone.

There was something about the girl's determination that seemed familiar . . .

I made a sudden decision.

"Let me ask him," I said.

I wasn't at all sure this contemporary of novelist Jack Kerouac and poet Allen Ginsberg — this much-honored icon of modern literature — wanted to spend his "down" time with a teen. But Ferlinghetti seemed to sense something too. His blue eyes lit up: "Sure, bring her in."

The girl rushed into Ferlinghetti's dressing room.

"Oh, Mr. Ferlinghetti, you were so wonderful tonight," she said, and then stopped, tongue-tied.

"Thank you," he said, smiling, and then he talked a bit, trying to put her at ease. His friends describe Ferlinghetti as a "very shy man," so it was quite something to see him work so hard, and so adroitly, to ease the young lady into conversation. Finally she said:

"Mr. Ferlinghetti, I want to give you this. Two years ago, a Border Voices poet came into our classroom and gave each of us a stone, or a leaf, or something else to write about. I got this stone. I wrote my first poem about it, and now poetry is a big part of my life, and I just love your poetry and . . . well, I want you to have this."

Ferlinghetti took the stone and admired it, promising to give it an honored place in his office.

Then the girl leaned down and kissed him on the top of his head.

"I love you," she said, and rushed from the room.

There's a lot you could say about Lawrence Ferlinghetti. For example: his *A Coney Island of the Mind* continues to be the most popular poetry book in the United States, having sold more than a million copies since it was first published in 1958. Or you could say: Ferlinghetti has exerted a powerful influence as author, critic, painter, owner of City Lights Books, and political gadfly.

In San Diego, they add one more thing: "that Ferlinghetti, man . . . he's got HEART."

The Bird*

And now our government
a bird with two right wings
flies on from zone to zone

And this year it's the Great Movie Cowboy
            in the cockpit
And next year it's the great Bush pilot
And now it's the Chameleon Kid
and he keeps changing the logo on
            his captain's cap
and now it's a donkey and now an elephant
and now some sort of crossbreed
with a donkey's head
And who knows who'll be pilot next

---

* Copyright © by Lawrence Ferlinghetti. The poem had its debut in the fourth Border Voices anthology (1997). It is reprinted here by permission of Lawrence Ferlinghetti.

("They're interchangeable, stupid")

And now we recognize two of the crew
who took out a contract on America
and one is a certain gringo wretch
who's busy monkeywrenching
crucial parts of the engine
and its life-support systems
while his sidekick a certain doleful
        Kansas cut-up
is cutting up the parts to jettison
and they got a big fat hose
to siphon off the fuel to privatized tanks
And all the while we just sit there
in the passenger seats
the clay population in rows
without parachutes
listening to all the news that's fit to air
over the one-way PA system
about how the contract on America
is really good for us and so on and so on

And so off into the wild blue yonder
of our postmodern
manifest   destiny.

Dragon's Teeth[*]

A headless man is running
down the street

He is carrying his head
in his hands
A woman runs after him
She has his heart
in her hands
The bombs keep falling
sowing hate
And they keep running
down the streets
Not the same two people
but thousands of others & brothers
All running
from the bombs that keep falling
sowing pure hate

And for every bomb that's dropped
up spring a thousand Bin Ladens
a thousand new terrorists
Like dragon's teeth sown
From which armed warriors sprang up
Crying for blood

As the smart bombs sowing hate
Keep falling and falling and falling

Amy Gerstler*
2003 Border Voices Poetry Fair

You know a poet is doing something right when they get a rave review in the *Los Angeles Times.* Listen to this:

"Gerstler has created a singular body of work, at once witty, daring, and full of pathos . . . she is the wisecracker in the face of the inexplicable."

Others agree. Of Gerstler's eight collections of poetry, one (*Crown of Weeds*) won a California Book Award, and another (*Bitter Angel*) was honored with a National Book Critics Circle Award, while 2000's *Medicine* was a finalist for the Phi Beta Kappa Award. Her most recent collection is *Ghost Girl* (Penguin, 2004)

A writer of nonfiction and journalism as well as poetry, Gerstler has written for the *Village Voice*, *Los Angeles Magazine*, the *Los Angeles Times*, *Art and Antiques*, and numerous other publications. Her writing has appeared in catalogs for art exhibitions at various museums and galleries including the Whitney Museum of American Art, the Los Angeles Museum of Con-

---

* Photo by Brian Tucker

temporary Art, the Fort Wayne Museum of Art in Indiana, and Brooke Alexander Gallery in New York.

In 1989, Gerstler collaborated with visual artist Alexis Smith on an exhibition and related artists book entitled *Past Lives.* This installation traveled to Josh Baer Gallery in New York City. Gerstler and Smith later collaborated on another exhibition, *The Sorcerer's Apprentice,* which was shown at the Miami Art Museum in 2000, and traveled to the Museum of Contemporary Art in San Diego in 2001.

Gerstler teaches in the fine arts department at Art Center College of Design in Pasadena, California, and is on the faculty of the writing seminars program at Bennington College in Vermont.

PERSONAL NOTE FROM THE EDITOR #2: It proved impossible to get timely permission from Amy Gerstler's publisher to reprint "Buddha Sonnet #1," the poem in the 2003 Border Voices anthology, so Amy sent us a few new ones to pick from.

What a lucky break for us! The poem "(dining)" is really funny, while "Tsunami" sent chills down the editorial spine. The grateful editor e-mailed Amy immediately:

> "Your poetry makes me feel like Ezra Pound felt in 1922. After reading/editing 'The Waste Land,' Pound wrote to Eliot: 'Complimenti, you bitch. I am wracked by the seven jealousies, and cogitating an excuse for always exuding my deformative

secretions in my own stuff, and never getting an outline. I go into nacre and objets d'art.'

To which Amy replied:

"Thanks for the 'complementi' " !

(dining)*

"The hope of dining well deceives you."
– Juvenal
(Whispered by a waiter into the ear of a customer he has just seated)

Our kitchen's grimy as a crypt.
Please pardon the grease
Where your centerpiece dripped.
Seahorse tartar is our special today,
But allow me to suggest for your entrée
Mutton soufflé, which tastes like lanolin,
Or cold ragout of pregnant terrapin,
Or fondue of kazoo and accordion —
A dish that polkas down your gullet...
Unless you prefer a plate of mullet
On a bed of al dente dental floss,
With a fried side of maidenhair moss
Grown only in spring,
Or plaid carpet samples á la king.
The jellied veal knuckle smelled rather tarry.

---

* Copyright © by Amy Gerstler. The poem, previously unpublished, is printed here with the permission of the author.

And we're out of gearshift sherbet. I'm sorry.
Our oysters in marmalade will make you weep.
The monkey's beard tea needs more time to
steep.
Our chef's previous job was shearing sheep,
Then she graduated to grooming horses.
During the last war she transported corpses.
She knows three ways to prepare red herrings
All with maraschino cherries and glazed ball
bearings.

Tsunami[*]

What caused us to set a course for shore days
ahead
of schedule? An abundance of strange things
floating
in the water. Unopened packages of ground
meat
and noodles. A straw hat with "Relax, It's Sim-
ple!"
stitched in loopy script on the brim. Amber bot-
tles
of prescription pills and expensive cosmetics.
Laminated menus from a seaside resort with pic-
tures
of shrimp and hot peppers *en brochette* cap-
tioned in four

190

languages. The text message our diver received from

his wife as we made our way back simply read
   disaster.

Or perhaps it was *catastrophe* she keyed in, and after

that the beautiful Japanese word for tidal wave.

The place we returned to is not the island we left.

The dock is gone.   Villages have disappeared. Dead

tourists still wear bathing suits, their bodies sunburnt

the color of cooked lobsters. I'm trying to remember

the Greek term for brotherly love. Is it *philios?* Please

let it be *philios.* I need a mantra to calm me each
   morning

as I exit my tent, a merciful word to repeat in my head.

Dana Gioia

2006 Border Voices Poetry Fair

A BRIEF BIOGRAPHY: Chairman of the National Endowment for the Arts, internationally acclaimed poet, controversial critic, former BBC commentator as well as one-time top executive for General Foods — whew!!! We're putting a period to this list of Dana Gioia's accomplishments not because we've run out of things to cite (he's also written opera libretti, for example) but because Gioia has frequently indicated that his primary love is poetry: "As long as humanity faces mortality and uses language to describe its existence, poetry will remain one of its essential spiritual resources" (from Gioia's *Disappearing Ink: Poetry at the End of Print Culture*). Gioia's poetry collection *Interrogations at Noon* won the American Book Award in 2002.

A FEW NOTES ABOUT THE POEM (AND A BIT MORE BIOGRAPHY): During his long and carefully crafted career, Dana Gioia has seemed, at times, to dominate contemporary literary discussions. His book *Can Poetry Matter?* ignited a firestorm by arguing that poetry has become marginalized in society, and that "the voluntary

192

audience of serious poetry consists mainly of poets, would-be poets, and a few critics."

Gioia welcomes and indeed frequently provokes outrage, in hopes that the ensuing controversy will generate not only discussion but art. After publication of another much-debated book (*California Poetry: From the Gold Rush to the Present*), Gioia co-editor Chryss Yost admitted that "We would love this book to lead to five other California anthologies in protest — that kind of dialogue is essential to creating a healthy environment."

The accompanying poem illustrates the Gioia tendency to provoke and amuse. On the surface, it is a delightful compilation of monetary nicknames and metaphors, revealing — with tongue firmly planted in cheek — the many ways money impacts our consciousness and viscera. It provokes us to think about money as evil, as friend, and as our constant companion along with its compatriots: greed, envy and the desire for comfort. The poem is also provoking to those who know that Gioia is a champion of formal poetry. It lacks the rhythm, rhyme, iambic pentameter, etc., that mark much of Gioia's verse. It's a puzzle, an oddity in the Gioia oeuvre, until — WAIT! The critical reader may suddenly notice that Gioia launched the poem in syllabic verse — five careful syllables per line — only to allow it to be HACKED into various multiples and divisions of five, under the pressure of — MONEY! It is form as metaphor, an in-joke for the cognoscenti, and as such, quintessentially Gioia.

193

Money[*]

Money is a kind of poetry.
— **Wallace Stevens**

Money, the long green,
cash, stash, rhino, jack
or just plain dough.

Chock it up, fork it over,
shell it out. Watch it
burn holes through pockets.

To be made of it! To have it
to burn! Greenbacks, double eagles,
megabucks and Ginnie Maes.

It greases the palm, feathers a nest,
holds heads above water,
makes both ends meet.

Money breeds money.
Gathering interest, compounding daily.
Always in circulation.

Money. You don't know where it's been,
but you put it where your mouth is.
And it talks.

Galway Kinnell*
1999 Border Voices Poetry Fair

"When Kinnell is at the top of his form, there is no better poet writing in America."
— **Richard Tillinghast**

Galway Kinnell is a poet of journeys, both physical and metaphorical. His career itself has been a journey from the dense formal poetry of his youth — stanzas, rhymes, and a sometimes stilted diction inspired by Milton via

Donne and Yeats — to the flowing, apocalyptic visions of his middle career, and, more recently, to poems as gently loving as anything in modern literature and to satire as funny and compelling as Jonathan Swift.

The literary historian David Perkins has described Kinnell as one of those poets who are "against civilization," and Kinnell himself, in an interview, alluded to the need for the poet to reject civilization's restrictions on self and percep-

---

* Photo by Bobbie Kinnell

tion in order to become one with nature, with reality and being:

"If you could keep going deeper and deeper," Kinnell said, "you'd finally not be a person . . . you'd be an animal; and if you kept going deeper and deeper, you'd be a blade of grass or ultimately perhaps a stone. And if a stone could speak, (poetry) would speak for it."

This approach operates most powerfully in Kinnell's poems "The Porcupine" and "The Bear," in which the poet becomes one with the animals he is writing about, sharing in their deaths and finding in those deaths "that sticky infusion, that rank flavor of blood, that poetry, by which I lived . . . "

Kinnell's heroes are the poets he reveres, such as William Carlos Williams, portrayed in one poem as throwing pearls of wisdom to a swinish audience of academics at some nameless university who pay him almost "total inattention . . . But you didn't even care . . . You seemed / Above remarking we were not your friends . . . In an hour / Of talking your honesty built a tower."

And, as alluded to above, Kinnell has found a refreshing tenderness of experience with his family, a tenderness reflected in his book *Mortal Act, Mortal Words*, from which the poem printed here was selected. It is a poem that can perhaps best be read as instructions from a father to his son, on how to cry.

More recently, Kinnell has cast off, in a sort of immense poetic shrug, some of the reservations of his earlier verse in order to discover a powerful satiric voice, one that can poke fun at academics ("The Deconstruction of Emily Dickinson") as well as the pomposities that veil the essential fragility of the human condition ("Holy Shit").

Kinnell was born in 1927 and grew up in Rhode Island. He did not start writing seriously until he was an undergraduate at Princeton where, under the influence of classmate W.S. Merwin, he became a devotee of Yeats, who seemed "not only the greatest of all poets, but also . . . poetry itself." He has won many prizes, including the Pulitzer and the National Book Award, and is currently a Chancellor of The Academy of American Poets.

Crying*

Crying only a little bit
is no use. You must cry
until your pillow is soaked!
Then you can get up and laugh.
Then you can jump in the shower
and splash-splash-splash!
Then you can throw open your window
and, "Ha ha! ha ha!"
And if people say, "Hey,
what's going on up there?"
"Ha ha!" sing back, "Happiness
was hiding in the last tear!
I wept it! Ha Ha!"

---

* "Crying" from *THREE BOOKS*. Copyright © 1993 by Galway Kinnell. Previously published in *Mortal Acts, Mortal Words* (1980). Reprinted by permission of the author. All rights reserved.

Steve Kowit

2001 Border Voices Poetry Fair

A Word of Explanation: The irrepressible Steve Kowit, having seen how Border Voices biographies are written, wanted to try writing his own. So here's Steve's "Bare-Bones Bio" and "More on Kowit," in which he ruthlessly dissects his own life. Our editorial comment follows immediately after.

BARE-BONES BIO: Steve Kowit is the author of several collections of poetry including *Lurid Confessions* (1983), *The Dumbbell Nebula* (2000), *The Gods of Rapture* (2006) and *The First Noble Truth* (forthcoming, 2007). He is also the author of the popular poetry manual *In the Palm of Your Hand* and of the first anthology in America to feature the work of thoroughly accessible poets, *The Maverick Poets*. He has won the State Street Poetry Prize, the Atlanta Review Poetry Prize, the Tampa Review Poetry Prize, The San Diego Literary Lights Life Time Achievement Award, a National Endowment for the Arts Poetry Fellowship, and two Pushcart Prizes. He teaches at Southwestern College in Chula Vista.

MORE ON KOWIT: Steve Kowit came of age in the New York poetry coffee-shops such as Le Metro and Les Deux Megots, but that was also the era of America's Black anti-racist revolution and an essential part of his education. Formally, he studied in New York with two contemporary masters: Robert Lowell and Stanley Kunitz. He then spent a few years in San Francisco during the heyday of that city's counterculture revolution in the mid-60s. If Hart Crane and Walt Whitman had been his earliest poetic heroes, he came to see Allen Ginsberg and Robinson Jeffers as the guiding spirits of a new visionary and politically conscious poetics and populist, thoroughly accessible aesthetic. After refusing to serve in Vietnam he spent three years living with his beloved wife Mary in Mexico, Central and South America avoiding the clutches of the genocidal US military. Returning to the States, he taught at community colleges in Idaho and Maryland, worked for a couple of years as a book editor in Florida, and then moved to San Diego where he became involved in the Gurdjieff, Vipassana and Zen communities. In response to being given the Zen koan Muji ("Do dogs have Buddha-nature") by one of his teachers, Kowit sat in meditation with the question for several months and then formed San Diego County's first animal rights movement.   After years of teaching poetry writing workshops he organized his thoughts and prejudices on the subject into the well-known teaching manual: *In the Palm of Your Hand: The Poet's Portable Workshop*, which remains, many years later, one of the most popular books on the subject. In recent years, like a number of other politically conscious American Jews, he has become a vociferous advocate for the rights of the Palestinian people.

OFFICIAL EDITORIAL COMMENT ON STEVE'S BIO: Good job, Steve.

UNOFFICIAL COMMENT: Steve left out that he is the sort of guy whose phone is always ringing off the hook with people needing advice or a shoulder to cry on or a friend to laugh with, all of which he is happy to provide. He ALSO left out how every page of his books, as the critic Ron Koertge said, "enchants or breaks my heart or makes me laugh. Or all three at once!"

The Blue Dress[*]

When I grab big Eddie, the gopher drops from
his   teeth,
& bolts for the closet, vanishing
into a clutter of shoes & valises & vacuum
    attachments
& endless crates of miscellaneous rubbish.
Grumbling & cursing, carton by carton,
I lug everything out:
that mountain of hopeless detritus — until,
with no place to hide, he breaks
for the other side of the room, & I have him at
last,

---

trapped in a corner, tiny & trembling.
I lower the plastic freezer bowl over his head &
                              Boom! —
slam the thing down.
                         "Got him!" I yell out,
slipping a folder under the edge for a lid.
But when I open the front door, it's teeming,
a rain so fierce it drives me back into the house,
& before I can wriggle into my sneakers,
Mary, impatient, has grabbed the contraption
out of my hands & run off into the yard with it,
   barefoot.
She's wearing that blue house dress.
I know just where she's headed: that big
mossy boulder down by the oleanders
across from the shed,
& I know what she'll do when she gets there —
hunker
down, slip off the folder,
let the thing slide to the ground
while she speaks to it softly, whispers
encouraging, comforting things.
Only after the gopher takes a few tentative steps,
dazed, not comprehending how he got back
to his own world, then tries to run off,
will she know how he's fared: if he's wounded,
or stunned, or okay — depraved ravisher
of our gladiolus & roses, but neighbor & kin
   nonetheless.
Big Eddie meows at my feet while I stand
by the window over the sink, watching
her run back thru the rain,
full of good news. Triumphant. Laughing.
Wind
lashing the trees. It's hard to fathom

how gorgeous she looks, running like that
through the storm: that blue
sheath of a dress aglow in the smoky haze —
that luminous blue dress pasted by rain to her
hips.
I stand at the window, grinning, amazed
at my own undeserved luck —
at a life that I still, when I think of it,
hardly believe.

Philip Levine*
1994 Border Voices Poetry Fair

"If Levine hadn't been a poet, he would have been dictator of the world. He knew the power of rhythm to move us. He could have been the greatest demagogue ever."
— **Glover Davis**
Poet, educator, and former
student of Philip Levine

A wealthy woman, a woman born into luxury, fingered her pearls and began to cry when she heard Philip Levine read his poem "They Feed They Lion," with its savage scorn for the arrogantly well-to-do, with its unforgiving prediction of a day of wrath:

Out of burlap sacks, out of bearing butter,
Out of the black bean and wet slate bread,
Out of the acids of rage, the candor of tar,
Out of creosote, gasoline, drive shafts, wooden dollies,
They Lion grow . . .

---

* Photo by Frances Levine.

From the oak turned to a wall, they Lion,
From they sack and they belly opened
And all that was hidden burning on the oil-stained
earth
They feed they Lion and he comes.

It was March 12, 1994, at the first Border Voices Poetry Fair in San Diego's Balboa Park, and Levine had everyone in the palm of his hand — had held them there since he took the stage, slumped and grey after a long plane ride from Fresno. Then he straightened up, his mustache bristling with miraculous energy, and complimented San Diego on its fine weather: "Fresno has its virtues too. The average temperature this month is over 100 degrees. After living there for 20 years, I know that I'm going to live forever — I'm completely dried up."

WHAM! That last line hits the crowd and they're charmed, they roar with laughter, and then Levine, that paragon of timing and rhythm, slams them with "They Feed They Lion" and the poem is like a dark cloud coming across the day, the lightning flickering . . .

Levine's mastery of rhythm is legendary. It is a mastery that comes from careful attention to the "voices" in his poems, as well as his extraordinary willingness to revise his work and even to discard poems he doesn't think are working.

In an interview in the May 1999 issue of *The Cortland Review*, Levine admitted that he throws away half the poems he writes, often because the "voice" isn't right. And he's delighted when a poem surprises him with a new voice: "If I know exactly what the voice is (in advance), then it's

usually a voice I've already used so many god-
damn times that I don't need another poem that
sounds just like it. I think in the best poems I
make a lot of discoveries about voice, about sub-
ject, about what my real feelings are."

Levine is the author of sixteen books of po-
etry, most recently *Breath* (Alfred A. Knopf,
2004). He has won numerous prizes, including
the Pulitzer Prize for *The Simple Truth* (1994).
He has also published a collection of essays, *The
Bread of Time: Toward an Autobiography* (1994),
edited *The Essential Keats* (1987), and co-edited
and translated two books: *Off the Map: Selected
Poems of Gloria Fuertes* (with Ada Long, 1984)
and *Tarumba: The Selected Poems of Jaime Sa-
bines* (with Ernesto Trejo, 1979).

For two years he served as chair of the Litera-
ture Panel of the National Endowment for the
Arts, and he was elected a Chancellor of The
Academy of American Poets in 2000. He cur-
rently lives in New York City and Fresno, and
teaches at New York University.

Innocence*

Smiling, my brother straddles a beer keg
outside a pub. 1944, a year
of buzz bombs. He's in the Air Corps,
on a mission to London to refill
oxygen tanks for B-24s, the flying coffins
as they were dubbed by those who flew

---

* Copyright @ 2006 by Philip Levine. Originally printed in
The Georgia Review, Spring 2006.

them night after night. Fifty years later
a German writer on a walking trip
through East Anglia meets a gardener
who recalls as a boy of twelve hearing
the planes taking off at dusk to level
the industrial cities of the Ruhr
and later, when the Luftwaffe was all
but destroyed, whatever they could reach.
"50,000 American lads died." The gardener
recalls waking near dawn, the planes
stuttering back in ones and twos.
How many Germans died we may
never know. "Must have been women,
children, and the very old what with
all the eligible men gone to war."
The German novelist writes it down
word for word in his mind and goes
on to an appointment with an English
writer born in Germany, a Jew
who got out in time. My brother
recalls a young woman who lived above
the pub, a blond, snapping the picture
outside the pub with his own Argus
C3, and points out a horse & wagon
around the corner loaded with beer kegs
but with no driver. The pub is closed,
for it is not long after dawn and the city
is rising for work and war. We call the time
innocent for lack of a better word, we call
all the Germans "the Nazis" because it suits
the vengeance we exact. Some hours later
the two writers born in Germany sit
out in a summer garden and converse
in their adopted tongue and say nothing
about what they can't forget as children,

for these two remain children until they die.
My brother, blind now, tells me he is glad
to be alive, he calls every painful day
a gift he's not sure he earned but accepts
with joy. He lives in a Neutra house
with entire walls of glass and a view
of the Pacific, a house he bought
for a song twenty years ago in disrepair.
He accepts the fact each year squadrons
of architectural students from Europe and Asia
drop in to view the place, and though
he cannot see he shows them around
graciously and lets them take
their photographs. When I tell him
of the 50,000 airmen the gardener told
the novelist about, his blind eyes
tear up, for above all my older brother
is a man of feeling, and his memory is precise—
like a diamond—and he says, "Not that many."

Genny Lim[*]
2000 Border Voices Poetry Fair

It must be fun to be Genny Lim.

After publishing two exquisite and powerful plays in 1989 and 1991, and an equally impressive collection of poetry (*Winter Place*, 1989), the San Francisco poet turned to performance poetry and the crafting of improvisatory works on-stage, backed by jazz musicians.

"There's something exciting about watching something occurring spontaneously in an improvisatory way," Lim said in a 1996 interview. "Cause you feel like you're part of history at that moment. It's not happening at any other place or time, and it's not happening in the past and it won't happen in the future."

Lim has won applause and awards for her performances, which rely on "the power of voice and demeanor (so that) another transmission occurs that you cannot negate or underestimate." In 1996, she was featured on PBS' "United States of Poetry," while in 2002 the documentary "The Voice: Genny Lim" premiered

---

[*] Photo by Bob Hsiang.

on PBS and at the San Francisco International Asian American Film Festival.

One of the problems with performance poetry, of course, is that it is not always as compelling when transferred from the stage — its natural home — to the page. Without the "call and response" of living voice and jazz riffs, an improvisatory poem can seem incomplete. But even that incompleteness has power, as compelling as the first dawn on the newly formed and still-chaotic ball-of-mud that became our Earth. Something is being born . . .

That momentous sense of birth, of dawn-world creation, is present in the poem printed here. After an initial burst of hip terminology, the poem accumulates power through a series of almost-biblical lists: lists of failures of communication and expectation ("There is no common language . . . no dharma among thieves" "Once lapis lazuli, the sea is sewage") and lists of impossible desires ("I want to stop time and / twist it open till it cries / I want to explode time and / twist it open til it cries") and then collapses into irony, the death of worlds (or at least the death of world-views, which irony pops and explodes like the sword of God): "Love was a hip invention / before language."

This is wonderful. Still, many of Lim's admirers confess nostalgia for the style of some of her earlier works, such as the play *Paper Angels*, which contains scenes as haunting and lyrical as any found on the American stage.

In addition to *Winter Place*, Lim has produced a second collection of poetry, *Child of War*. She is the author of a children's book, *Wings for Lai*

Ho, and she co-authored *ISLAND: Poetry and History of Chinese Immigrants on Angel Island, 1910-1940.*

Lim can be heard on Jon Jang's 1997 CD Soul Note release, "Immigrant Suite," and on Asian Improv's CD "Devotee" with Francis Wong and the late Glenn Horiuchi. She has performed with such notable artists as Max Roach, Tootie Heath, Eddie Marshall and Herbie Lewis.

A Hip Invention[*]

Trying to find satori in the '90s was
like driving blind
You had the wheel but you
didn't know where you were going

Love is a hip invention
A twenty first century novelty
There is no common language among birds, men
or   trees
No dharma among thieves or postmodern sutras
Computer mantras come in innovative software
and
human emotions are stimulated by profit
Out here, the seven hills overlooking the Bay
rise
like seven gaudy Buddhas
Once lapis lazuli, the sea is sewage

There is no nuclear path to enlightenment
without sacrificial death
No cross between obsidian and light without
pain

Native peoples worshipped the Eagle who flew
into the sun to bring us back the light
we are the sun which brings the light
We think we are the drum which beats the world
alive
We think we are the world which nature must
survive
But the millennium drones with the expulsions
of
missiles, tanks and uzis
as we recite out children's names
Hiroshima, Bay of Pigs, El Salvador, Persian
Gulf . . .
Fingering our memories like rosaries
O holy trinity of technocracy!
E pluribus unum
Capital, profit and consumption

I want to stop time and
twist it open till it cries
I want to explode time and
twist it open till it cries
I want to explode time because it's stuck and
I am stuck in it
I am stuck and you are stuck
We are stuck and
our children are stuck
in needles and veins

211

We are stuck
inside the barrel of a gun
inside a whiskey bottle and piss
inside pregnant bellies and perfume
inside the graffiti
inside sex
inside the ozone
inside monkey talk and think tanks
inside white skin
inside self-hate
inside death
inside money
inside shit
inside a condom of reality
inside a dysfunctional family
inside our bodies
inside our being
inside ourselves
inside this White House of
America

Love was a hip invention
before language

Sandra McPherson*

2003 Border Voices Poetry Fair

It can be argued that the most perceptive critics — or at least the harshest judges — of a poet are his or her fellow poets. If that's true, then Sandra McPherson must be very good indeed. Listen, for example, to Pulitzer Prize-winning poet Anthony Hecht:

> *(McPherson) has flung down and danced upon most of her competition. . . . a genuine poet.*

Another test is to use your spinal cord as a divining rod. If you feel a thrill coursing along it as you read a poem — if there's an electrical vibration that begins in the nape of the neck and spreads down the spine and through the shoulders and down to the fingertips — then, by gawd, you've just read a POEM! And again and again, lines in Sandra McPherson's poetry achieve that effect . . .

---

* Photo by Henry Carlile

As they do in "One Way She Spoke to Me" — even if you DON'T know the sad and inspiring story behind it.

Try it. Read the poem now, before I tell you what life event prompted it. Do you feel the mystery that begins in that first stanza . . . the question about WHO it is who can't raise their voice, can't whisper? The mystery that grows as snails spell slurred words in silver trails on the front door, a mystery that reaches out to embrace all of us in those wonderful five lines at the end? We somehow know, without being directly told, that this is a story rooted in the failure to communicate; and we are convinced, once again, that such failures lie somewhere close to the heart of all human tragedy . . .

The poem is from *The Spaces Between Birds*, the 1996 collection that deals with McPherson's relationship with her then-29-year-old daughter Phoebe. Phoebe was born with Asperger's Syndrome, a form of autism.

"She doesn't understand social signals," said McPherson. "She's kind of proud of this ... of this different kind of mind." As a child, Phoebe had difficulty talking the way other people do. She spoke in metaphors, she had a hard time with pronouns. And once, she wrote a note in snails on the front door.

It didn't work. The snails moved. And soon after that a poem was born. And it still sends chills down the spine.

Raised in California, Sandra McPherson studied at the graduate level with Elizabeth Bishop and David Wagoner at the University of Washington. Her poetry collections include *A Visit to*

Civilization (Wesleyan University Press, 2002), *The Edge Effect* (1996), *The God of Indeterminacy* (1993), and *The Year of Our Birth* (1978, which was nominated for the National Book Award. Her poems have appeared in *The New Yorker*, *The Yale Review*, *The Paris Review*, *Poetry*, *The Southern Review* and *TriQuarterly*.

Among other honors, she has received two grants from the Ingram Merrill Foundation, three National Endowment for the Arts fellowships, a Guggenheim Foundation Fellowship, and an award in literature from the American Academy and Institute of Arts and Letters. Her poetry was featured in the PBS special "The Language of Life," hosted by Bill Moyers.

She teaches creative writing and poetry-as-literature courses at the University of California at Davis, where she has been on the faculty since 1985.

One Way She Spoke to Me[*]

I would say, "Whisper." And she could
never figure how to do it. I would say
"Speak louder," into the phone, nor
could she raise her voice.

But then I found such a whisper, the trail
as she began to write to me in snails,

---

[*] Copyright © by Sandra McPherson.   Reprinted, by permission of the author, from *The Spaces Between Birds*, Wesleyan University Press, 1996.

215

in silver memos on the front door,
in witnesses to her sense of touch.

Home late, I found them slurred
and searching, erasing the welcome
she'd arranged them in:
H — twelve snails. I — seven or six.

They were misspelling it,
digressing in wayward caravans and pileups,
mobile and rolling but with little perspective,
their eyestalks smooth as nylons on tiny legs.

I raised her in isolation. But it is these snails
who keep climbing the walls. For them, maybe
every vertical makes an unending tree —
and every ascension's lovely.

Why else don't they wend homeward to ground?
But what do we do? We are only a part
of a letter in a word. And we are on our
bellies   with   speech,   wondering,   wondering
slowly,

how to move toward one another.

Fred Moramarco

1994 and 1995 Border Voices Poetry fairs

Sometimes it seems as if Fred Moramarco (AKA "Federico" among lovers of Italian cookery) is EVERYWHERE.

Type his name into Google and you'll find him:

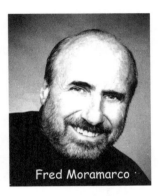

Fred Moramarco

(a) **Splashed across** the top of the official Raymond Carver Web site, where you are advised to read his penetrating and loving essay about the great fiction writer.

(b) **On amazon.com,** where you can buy his two best-selling Italian cookbooks.

(c) **Reviewing a new poetry collection** for *The American Poetry Review.*

(d) **Getting a glowing write-up** for directing a new play — or <u>appearing</u> in one!!

(e) Or **publishing** some of his own poetry.

Brilliant and seemingly omnipresent, Moramarco nevertheless outdid himself on April 4, 1994. That's when he appeared before a crowd of 40,000 at the home opener of the Padres baseball team, and proceeded to read an original poem saluting outfielder/superstar Tony Gwynn. The crowd cheered, the stadium rocked

217

— and poetry achieved a level of notoriety in San Diego from which it has never fully recovered . . .

Moramarco's appearance was arranged by the Border Voices Poetry Project as part of its ongoing effort to showcase poetry in San Diego and elsewhere. Federico has continued to promote poetry, Border Voices and good Italian cooking ever since. Here, in more traditional form, is his biography:

Fred Moramarco is Editor of *Poetry International*, published at San Diego State University where he teaches American Literature and Creative Writing. He co-edited *The Poetry of Men's Lives: An International Anthology,* published in 2005 by the University of Georgia Press. With his son Stephen he wrote *Italian Pride: 101 Reasons to Be Proud You're Italian* and has just published a sequel, *Deliciously Italian: From Sunday Supper to Special Occasions/101 Recipes to Share and Enjoy.* He is also the co-author of *Containing Multitudes: Poetry in the United States Since 1950* as well as *Modern American Poetry,* and co-editor of *Men of Our Time: Male Poetry in Contemporary America.* His poems and essays have appeared in many periodicals and online journals including *American Poetry Review, The Literary Review, Poetry East, 88, A Journal of Contemporary Poetry, The Nation, ForPoetry.com, Vocabula.com* and many others. His own chapbooks include *Last Minute Adjustments, Act Three and Other Poems, Love and Other Dark Matters* and *One Hundred and Eighty Degrees.* He has taught in and administered the San Diego London Semester program twice (and will do so again in Spring 2007) and has recently attended international conferences in Sevilla, Cabo San Lucas and Genoa. He gave the plenary address at the Italian North American Studies conference in Genoa in 2001.

Professor Moramarco is also involved in the San Diego Theater scene. He is an actor and the Artistic Director of Laterthanever Productions, a theater company he founded in 2002 dedicated to producing plays dealing with important social issues. He produced and directed A.R. Gurney's *Mrs. Farnsworth*, a play related to the 2004 election, and in June 2006 he co-produced *Hannah & Martin*, a play by Kate Fodor about the relationship between Hannah Arendt and Martin Heidegger. He recently performed in Diversionary Theater's *Twilight of the Golds* and in Sledgehammer Theater's *A Patriot Act: The Trial of George W. Bush.*

Padres 94: A Diamond Vision[*]

Here on this diamond, baseball blossoms
each spring like a new love affair,
carrying memories of past seasons,
a hope chest filling the spring air
with smells of leather and pine tar,
conjuring images of unforgettable moments:
the sharp crack of wood against leather,
the cheering crowds, the bellowing organ.

Here on this diamond, we launch
a new season of promise and possibility.
This time in this place, a new team debuts —
Last year was a time for the Phillies and Jays,
who thrilled us in fall with remarkable plays,
but this year we'll watch as the Padres rebound,
on the tenth anniversary of the '84 team
who turned this field into magical ground . . .

This diamond's been home for Randy Jones and
    Gaylord Perry,
Rollie Fingers, Goose Gossage, Dave Winfield,
Willie McCovey, Ozzie Smith and Dave Dravecky
—

these players and more with heart and skill,
but none we've loved more than our own Tony
Gwynn.
He'll lead this young team being just who he is:
a player for us and for the ages, who carries
what's best

---

[*] The photo was snapped by Barbara Bowen-Doty. "Pa-
dres 94" is Copyright © Fred Moramarco.

about this amazing summer game into the
hearts of us   all.

On this diamond, this day, we salute Tony
Gwynn:
now on with the game, let the season begin!

Familiar Sensations*

Winter's different this year,
but I recognize it all the same,
the puffy grey clouds lasting deeper into the day,
the early darkness here before the light takes
hold.

Summer's just a blurred band of endless heat,
and spring's so far away it seems a different life.
I'll settle into winter clothes gladly and walk
the barren streets no matter what.

I won't be done in by the seasons.
All this has come and gone before
and will again despite how well
my paltry schemes delay the simple truth.

What that truth is, who will say?
A day's a day, a night's a night,
a week's a week, a year's a year —
wonderful inventions, circus tents

filled with sold out crowds, children hoisted on

---

* Copyright © Fred Moramarco

shoulders,
acrobats flying through the falsely lit air.

At the Garage Sale[*]

At the garage sale I went to last Saturday,
boxes and boxes of cassette tapes,
the music of their owners' lives,
lay strewn across the sidewalk like blood
splattered from a crime scene.
And there were books, cartons of them,
carrying memories of nights in soft chairs
to the unforgiving asphalt of the street.
There were cups and pots,
whole evenings of lingering meals,
whole 4th of July picnics, thanksgiving dinners
settled in kettles and roasting pans
that now seemed rusted and still,
like the overused grill,
sitting in the corner,
waiting for somebody to offer a buck.

At the garage sale I went to last Saturday,
there were children searching through boxes of
    yesterday's toys,
mothers sifting through piles of clothing on the
porch.
There were artists looking for frames,
teachers looking for classroom games,

---

beggars needing shoes with full soles,
athletes seeking a well-worn mitt,
and others wanting something to surprise them
in what's left behind by the people who change
lives,
who move on in the world
to the next astonishing adventure
that rushes by you like a comet,
unless you stop and stay still, watching
the silent blaze it makes in the sky,
trailing, not only clouds of glory, but of love.

Naomi Shihab Nye[*]
2001 Border Voices Poetry Fair

"In the current literary scene, one of the most heartening influences is the work of Naomi Shihab Nye . . . Reading her work enhances life."
— **William Stafford**, noted poet

"THE EDITOR IS DE-LIGHTED TO RE-TRACT": Every once in a while — a LONG while, I hope — the editor of this anthology is forced to admit that he has been an idiot. That his former opinion about someone or their writing was completely off-base.

This is one of those occasions.

Back in 2001, when we brought Naomi Shihab Nye to San Diego for the eighth annual Border Voices Poetry Fair, I wrote of how delighted I was with much of her work: that she had "a clear eye for detail and a resilient optimism,"

---

[*] Photo by Ha Lam

etc., etc. But then I began worrying aloud: had she REALLY mastered the art of writing memorable lines, of "enchanting words into forms resistant to time," as Zbigniew Herbert put it.

My inability to hear the haunting music in Nye's poetry was astonishing. It took quite an untrained ear to miss the beauty of lines like this, from her collection *Fuel* (1999):

> We who were driving north on that road
> pulled the car over, pulled it over
> because the grasses in their lanky goldenness
> called for standing alongside them
> while the whole sky
> held.

Oh well. My only excuse is that I was overly impressed with <u>formal</u> poetry at that time, and thought it would be good for Border Voices students to be reminded, frequently, about the time-honored techniques for writing memorable rhythms . . . I failed to see that, with the advances in poetic technique as well as changes in audience expectation, the beautiful repetitions of lines like "pulled the car over, pulled it over / because" can be just as effective as anything Yeats penned . . .

My tin ear became the target of vitriol from Naomi's fans. And she has LOTS of fans some of them very notable indeed, as the quote that leads off this biography indicates. She has earned those fans both because of the quality of her work, and because of the kindness of her nature — kindness that was displayed when she was invited to contribute to this book.

She wrote back GRANTING permission, adding:

> This is particularly touching to me since I recall the startling program notes at the San Diego festival saying my work was so forgettable — but hey, at least one person recalled one poem!

To which the editor replied:

> I can't imagine who could write such a stupid program note . . . One can only hope they have been suitably chastised by time . . . (as I have). Thank you for letting us reprint your fine poem.

Naomi concluded this exchange with typical graciousness:

> We are all chastised by time, indeed! Only wish our politicians would be — in quicker time!

Naomi Shihab Nye is the author and/or editor of more than twenty volumes. Her books of poetry include *19 Varieties of Gazelle: Poems of the Middle East*, *Red Suitcase*, *Words Under the Words*, *Fuel*, and *You & Yours* (2005). Nye has been a Lannan Fellow, a Guggenheim Fellow, and a Wittner Bynner Fellow (Library of Congress). She has received, among other honors, a Lavan Award from the Academy of American Poets, four Pushcart Prizes, and numerous awards and citations for her children's literature, including two Jane Addams Children's Book

Awards and the Isabella Gardner Poetry Award for 2005 for *You & Yours.* She has been featured on two PBS poetry specials — "The Language of Life with Bill Moyers" and "The United States of Poetry" — and also appeared on the weekly news program *NOW with Bill Moyers.*

Jerusalem

> *"Let's be the same wound if we must bleed.*
> *Let's fight side by side, even if the enemy*
> *is ourselves: I am yours, you are mine."*
> **— Tommy Olofsson**, Sweden

I'm not interested in
who suffered the most.
I'm interested in
people getting over it.

Once when my father was a boy
a stone hit him on the head.
Hair would never grow there.
Our fingers found the tender spot
and its riddle: the boy who has fallen
stands up. A bucket of pears
in his mother's doorway welcomes him home.
The pears are not crying.
Later his friend who threw the stone
says he was aiming at a bird.
And my father starts growing wings.

Each carries a tender spot:
something our lives forgot to give us.
A man builds a house and says,
"I am native now."
A woman speaks to a tree in place
of her son. And olives come.
A child's poem says,
"I don't like wars,
they end up with monuments."
He's painting a bird with wings
wide enough to cover two roofs at once.

Why are we so monumentally slow?
Soldiers stalk a pharmacy:
big guns, little pills.
If you tilt your head just slightly
it's ridiculous.

There's a place in my brain
where hate won't grow.
I touch its riddle: wind, and seeds.
Something pokes us as we sleep.

It's late but everything comes next.

Sharon Olds*
2000 and 2006 Border Voices Poetry fairs

BARE-BONES BIO: She is a writer who revels in lovable paradoxes, and her reticent honesty (more on THAT paradox in a minute) has made Sharon Olds one of the most popular poets  in the United States. Who else — to take one example — could melt the hearts of readers by describing the beauty of her body as it is parched by age, the tired flesh "withery and scrawny, and I like its silvery / witheriness, the skin thinning, / surface of a lake crimped by wind . . ." Olds's slightly off-kilter insights have garnered numerous honors, including a National Book Critics Circle Award. She has authored eight books of poetry, from *Satan Says* (1980) to *Strike Sparks: Selected Poems 1980-2002* (2004), and she currently teaches poetry workshops at New York University's Graduate Creative Writing Program. "Sharon Olds's poems are pure fire in the hands" (Michael Ondaatje, novelist).

---

* Photo by Catherine Mauger

A FEW NOTES ABOUT THE POEMS (AND A BIT MORE BIOGRAPHY): First things first: if you're like the editor of this volume, you had to throw open the dictionary when you reached the word "rhyparographer" in the poem "The Unswept." There you discovered that a "rhy`pa*rog"ra*ph-er" is someone who paints "foul or mean objects," and you have yet another clue to the paradox and triumph of Sharon Olds's career. Her poetry is filled with beauty, but it is not afraid to exhibit the stitches in a woman's body after childbirth, or to imagine her dead father rowing her enemies and finally herself into the afterlife. The poems, over the years, have grown as she has, and they have the appearance of being a faithful, though exceptionally vivid, recounting of her life (including frightening images of an alcoholic, dominating father and a cruel mother; childbirth; a kid blowing bubbles in milk; and — in the poem "The Prepositions" — the "Black / plump goof-off" in junior high "who walked past and / suddenly flicked my sweater-front"). But in a rare interview with the editor of this anthology, she resolutely refused to confirm that the stories are autobiographical, describing them instead as "apparently personal." Pressed for an explanation, she said that questions of loyalty and betrayal are important to her: "On the loyalty side is silence, and out toward this end of the spectrum is absolute silence, the poems not written . . . a kind of spiritual suicide . . . on the other side of the spectrum is song, and perhaps at the far end very little consideration for other people's privacy ... a kind of spiritual murder." In her poems, she says, she tries to find the truth, the sort of truth that will draw "the language angels who fly around the city looking for places to land," without betraying those she loves. And she writes incessantly, on buses, trains, planes, jotting notes on the back of her hand, preparing "fancies of crumbs / from under love's table." She is delighted, she says, when the poem finally "separates from you," like a bubble floating off from a little bubble pipe, and her poem "The Unswept" is a celebration of that act of artistic conception, conservation, and letting go.

LITTLE EXERCISE: In that 1991 interview quoted above, Olds also said that almost ALL of her poems are based on the four-beat line of the Episcopalian hymnal. See if you can find echoes of that in "The Unswept" and "The Prepositions."

Just to get you started, we'll scan the first two lines of "The Unswept" in exactly the same way that we would scan a line from a hymn.

Here's are two lines from a hymn, with the beat marked:

> We **will** not **fear**, for **God** hath **willed**
> His **truth** to **tri**umph **through** us.

And here are the first two lines of "The Unswept":

> **Brok**en **bay** leaf. **Ol**ive **pit**.
> **Crab** leg. **Claw**. **Cray**fish **arm**or

Have fun!

The Prepositions[*]

When I started Junior High, I thought
I'd probably be a Behavior Problem
all my life, John Muir Grammar
the spawning grounds, the bad-seed bed, but
the first morning at Willard, the dawn
of seventh grade, they handed me a list
of forty-five prepositions, to learn
by heart. I stood in the central courtyard,
enclosed garden that grew cement,
my pupils followed the line of the arches
up and over, up and over, like
alpha waves, *about, above,*
across, along, among, around, an
odd comfort began, in me,
before, behind, below, beneath,
beside, between, I stood in that sandstone
square, and started to tame. *Down,*
from, in, into, near, I was
located there, watching the Moorish half-
circles rise and fall. *Off,*
on, onto, out, outside, we
came from sixth grades all over the city
to meet each other for the first time,
White tennis-club boys who did not
speak to me, White dorks
who did, Black student-council guys who'd gaze
off, above my head, and the Black
plump goof-off, who walked past and

---

* Reprinted by permission of the author. From the book
Blood, Tin, Straw © 1999, Alfred A. Knopf, Inc.
232

suddenly flicked my sweater-front, I thought to
shame me.
Over, past, since, through,
that was the year my father came home in the
middle of the night with those thick earthworms
of blood on his face, trilobites of
elegant gore, cornice and crisp
waist of the extinct form,
till, to, toward, under, the
lining of my uterus convoluted,
shapely and scarlet as the jointed leeches
of wound clinging to my father's face in that
mask, *unlike, until, up,* I'd
walk, day and night, into
the Eden of the list, *hortus enclosus* where
everything had a place. I was *in*
relation to, upon, with, and when I
got to forty-five I could start over,
pull the hood of the list down over
my brain again. It was the first rest
I had had from my mind. My glance would run
slowly along the calm electro-
cardiogram of adobe cloister,
within, without, I'd repeat the prayer I'd
received, a place in the universe,
meaningless but a place, an exact location —
Telegraph, Woolsey, Colby, Russell —
Berkeley, 1956,
fourteen, the breaking of childhood, beginning
    of memory.

The Unswept[*]

Broken bay leaf. Olive pit.
Crab leg.   Claw. Crayfish armor.
Whelk shell. Mussel shell. Dogwinkle. Snail.
Wishbone tossed unwished on. Test
of sea urchin. Chicken foot.
Wrasse skeleton. Hen head,
eye shut, beak open as if
singing in the dark. Laid down in tiny
tiles, by the rhyparographer,
each scrap has a shadow — each shadow cast
by a different light. Permanently fresh
husks of the feast! When the guest has gone,
the morsels dropped on the floor are left
as food for the dead — O my characters,
my imagined, here are some fancies of crumbs
from under love's table.

Robert Pinsky[*]

1998 Border Voices Poetry Fair

"All art is quite useless."
— Oscar Wilde

Robert Pinsky loves language SO much: he savors its rough roots (the Germanic gutter-snarls and growls echoing beneath modern English) as much as he loves its soaring grace notes. It is this love that is reflected in the accompanying poem, which celebrates the endearing paradoxes of the language that binds and divides us

("That it is visible, invisible, dark and clear" and so on).

What may not be immediately obvious, unless you step WAY back from the poem, is that it is also a very short tribute, an act of compassionate admiration for those who — although deaf and/or blind — can still achieve insight and art. It is thus a celebration not only of language, but

---

[*] Boston University photo services

of the heroism displayed by the fragile, which is all of us.

And as such it gives the lie to the Oscar Wilde aphorism above, a much-quoted bit of nonsense uttered by the Irish playwright while he was in a VERY bad mood. When not suffering from an emotional hangover, Wilde was MUCH more forthcoming about the central role of art in guiding human affairs, noting that "Life imitates art far more than art imitates Life," and "It is through art, and through art only, that we can realise our perfection."

It is an insight that is embodied in the poem printed here, and it is an insight that has apparently inspired Pinsky throughout his admirable and useful career as poet, professor and (from 1997-2000) Poet Laureate of the United States.

It may seem odd to describe a great poet as useful — but in fact ALL great writing is useful, whether it be Plato's *Dialogues* or Shakespeare's plays — both of which nourish wisdom as well as insight into human affairs. In the same way, Yeats' poems feed the imagination and sensitize the ear, while Francis Bacon's essays help us to think and live WELL . . .

Pinsky's work is useful in just that way. A few examples (which is all we have room for) include:

1) Pinsky's fourth book of poems, *The Want Bone*, dealt with the chameleon-like nature of the modern intellectual — his / her ability to adopt numerous personas and belief-systems, all of them potent, none of them absolute — and helped us see how to live with this purgatorial and often exhilarating uncertainty.

2) While he was Poet Laureate, Pinsky was bombarded with requests to appear on TV shows and at various art events. He guided himself by what was <u>useful</u>. For example, as he told an interviewer for *Meridian* magazine: "There will be some things that just seem as though this is what the post was created for, something that involves encouraging somebody who's doing a very good job, bringing poetry into schools or something where you want to encourage and support something that's very worthy."

Robert Pinsky is the author of six books of poetry: *Jersey Rain* (Farrar, Straus & Giroux, 2000); *The Figured Wheel: New and Collected Poems 1966-1996* (1996), which won the 1997 Lenore Marshall Poetry Prize and was a Pulitzer Prize nominee; *The Want Bone* (1990); *History of My Heart* (1984); *An Explanation of America* (1980); and *Sadness and Happiness* (1975).

In 1999 he co-edited *Americans' Favorite Poems: The Favorite Poem Project Anthology* with Maggie Dietz (W.W. Norton & Company, Inc.). He has also published four books of criticism, including *The Sounds of Poetry* (Farrar, Straus, and Giroux, 1998), which was a finalist for the National Book Critics Circle Award; two books of translation, including *The Inferno of Dante* (1994), which received the Los Angeles Times Book Prize; and a computerized novel, *Mindwheel* (1985).

His honors include an American Academy of Arts and Letters award, *Poetry Magazine*'s Oscar Blumenthal prize, the William Carlos Williams Award, and a Guggenheim Foundation fellowship. He is currently poetry editor of the weekly

Internet magazine *Slate*. Pinsky teaches in the graduate writing program at Boston University.

If You Could Write One Great Poem, What Would You Want It to Be About?*

(Asked of four student poets at the Illinois Schools for the Deaf and Visually Impaired)

Fire: because it is quick, and can destroy.
Music: place where anger has its place.
Romantic Love — the cold or stupid ask why.
Sign: that it is a language, full of grace,

That it is visible, invisible, dark and clear,
That it is loud and noiseless and is contained
Inside a body and explodes in air
Out of a body to conquer from the mind.

238

Leroy V. Quintana
1994 Border Voices Poetry Fair

In Leroy Quintana's poems "a bitter-sweet but compassionate voice breaks through stones of silence . . ."
— Antonio C. Márquez

Leroy V. Quintana can smack you RIGHT between the eyes in just the SWEETEST way ... just listen (for example) to the shyly seductive voice in this neat little 1999 poem:

It was about 1958 or so when we finally got a phone, but the only girl I had enough nerve to call was the one who seemed to whisper, faithfully as well as exactly, what time it was, any time I called.
— from *The Great Whirl of Exile*

Or take another rhythmic gem from the same spectacular collection of poetry. Again, listen to the VOICE: this time, however, what you'll be listening for is the rumble of a subterranean anger.

The poem is called "The Rockets' Red Glare," and in it Quintana draws a little picture: the Super Bowl has come to San Diego, the rich are

239

rubbing shoulders with Bob Hope, and "we get fireworks." The poem continues:

> The woman behind me asks her son
> how so many rockets can be set off in succession.
>
> You just hire a bunch of Mexicans to run around
> with a lot of matches.
>
> Isn't it great, she sighs, bombs bursting in air,
> to be an American?

In an interview, Quintana said that "in many ways, I'm still basically a small-town New Mexican boy carrying on the oral tradition," and he also described his poems as "snapshots." Both things are true — Quintana was raised by his Mexican grandparents in small-town New Mexico, and the long nights were filled with folk tales (*cuentos*). From those stories, and also probably from his two years in Vietnam, he learned how to get quickly to the point, to avoid wasting words and time.

But Quintana also has a Hemingway-like ability to choose exactly the right series of images and intonations to create emotion. It is a talent that has drawn the praise of perceptive writers such as Yusef Komunyakaa, who himself won the Pulitzer Prize for *Neon Vernacular: New and Selected Poems*:

> Leroy Quintana has given us this tapestry of small moments that explode and fragment. His poetry seems to have been written through old eyes, a mature heart, with a perspective untouched by the contemporary flare for ego and surface intellect ... These are poems where the

various characters walk out of the white space to assume a real life. There's flesh on each metaphor.

Leroy V. Quintana is the winner of two American Book Awards. He is the author of *La Promesa and Other Stories* (University of Oklahoma Press, 2002) and six books of poetry, including *Hijo del Pueblo* (1976), *Sangre* (1981), *Interrogations* (1992), *The History of Home* (1993) and *My Hair Turning Gray Among Strangers* (1996).

He is a Professor of English at San Diego Mesa College

Padrino*

Uncle Leo, my padrino, was the very best of uncles.
He must have given me a million haircuts.
A quiet man, a boxing champion in the Army,
but I never knew him to use violence,
spoke to me harshly only once.
His advice always: be careful,
learn to be yourself.
I listened, in complete agreement.
But I seemed determined to undo my life.
Uncle Leo, who taught me how to use a saw.
Never, he said, go against the grain.

---

* Copyright © by Leroy V. Quintana. Reprinted by permission of the author.

Adrienne Rich[*]

1996 & 2004 Border Voices Poetry fairs

A NOTE FROM THE EDITOR: In the 1970s and 1980s, Adrienne Rich was one of the brighter suns hovering over creative writing programs throughout the United States. Her ardent feminism excited women poets as well as sympathetic males. The way she so elegantly mixed the ghost of iambic pentameter with her free-verse excursions (as in "Diving into the Wreck") delighted those who hungered for form and musicality in poetry, while her intense concern with discerning what was of real value in our fluid society was an inspiration to all those struggling with similar issues — including the editor of this anthology. If anything, Rich's influence has increased in recent years. She continues to provoke hero-worship in many young writers, and to enrich all of us.

A SOMEWHAT-TRADITIONAL BIO: Adrienne Rich is one of this country's most distinguished

---

[*] Photo by Lilian Kemp

poets. Her poetry is taught in English and women's studies courses across the country, and she is a revered teacher and activist. Since receiving the Yale Younger Poets Award in 1951 at the age of 21, she has not stopped writing in her distinctive voice, and in a language that incites action and provokes deliberation — about poverty, racism, sexism, violence, love between women, problems of survival, isolation and marginality.

One of her admirers, the much-honored poet W.S. Merwin, summed it up this way: "All her life (Adrienne Rich) has been in love with the hope of telling utter truth, and her command of language from the first has been startlingly powerful."

Rich is the recipient of numerous awards and honors: the 1999 Lannan Foundation Lifetime Achievement Award; the Ruth Lilly Poetry Prize; the Common Wealth Award in Literature; the National Book Award; the 1996 Tanning Award for Mastery in the Art of Poetry (the Wallace Stevens Award); and a MacArthur Fellowship. In 2003, she was awarded the Bollingen Prize for Poetry.

She is the author of numerous volumes of poetry, including *Diving into the Wreck* (1973); *The Dream of a Common Language* (1978); *The Fact of a Doorframe: Selected Poems 1950-2001*; and *Fox* (W.W. Norton, Fall 2001). Her 2004 collection of poems, *The School Among the Ruins*, was honored with the National Book Critics Circle Award and was chosen as one of *Library Journal*'s Best Poetry picks of 2004.

She has also authored five books of non-fiction prose, including *Of Woman Born: Motherhood as Experience and Institution* and *What is Found There: Notebooks on Poetry and Politics* (updated edition Fall 2003). Her most recent book of essays is entitled *Arts of the Possible: Essays and Conversations* (W.W. Norton, 2002). She also edited Muriel Rukeyser's *Selected Poems* for the Library of America (2004).

In the fall of 2006, Adrienne Rich was awarded the Medal for Distinguished Contribution to American Letters by the National Book Foundation. The judges articulated this distinction as follows: "Adrienne Rich . . . in recognition of her incomparable influence and achievement as a poet and nonfiction writer. For more than fifty years, her eloquent and visionary writings have shaped the world of poetry as well as feminist and political thought."

She is a former chancellor of the Academy of American Poets.

Messages*

I love the infinity of these silent spaces
Darkblue shot with deathrays but only a short
   distance
Keep of course water and batteries, antibiotics
Always look at California for the last time

We weren't birds, were we, to flutter past each
other
But what were we meant to do, standing or lying
down
Together on the bare slope where we were driven
The most personal feelings become historical

Keep your hands knotted deep inside your
sweater
While the instruments of force are more credible
than   beauty
Inside a glass paperweight dust swirls and set-
tles (Manzanar)
Where was the beauty anyway when we shoul-
dered   past each other

Where is it now in the hollow lounge

---

* "Messages" from *Fox: Poems 1998-2000* by Adrienne
Rich. Copyright © 2001 by Adrienne Rich. Used by per-
mission of the author and W.W. Norton & Company, Inc.

NOTE: Blaise Pascal (1623-1662): Le silence éternel de
ces espaces m'affraye. (The eternal silence of these infinite
spaces frightens me). See Pensées of Blaise Pascal, trans.
W.F. Trotter, Everyman's Library no. 874 (London: Dent,
1948), p. 61.

Of the grounded airline where the cameras
For the desouling project are being handed out
Each of us instructed to shoot the others naked

If you want to feel the true time of our universe
Put your hands over mine on the stainless pelvic
    rudder
No, here (sometimes the most impassive ones
will shudder)
The infinity of these spaces comforts me
Simple textures falling open like a sweater

Dreamwood[*]

In the old, scratched, cheap wood of the typing
stand
there is a landscape, veined, which only a child
can see
or the child's older self,
a woman dreaming when she should be typing
the last report of the day. If this were a map,
she thinks, a map laid down to memorize
because she might be walking it, it shows
ridge upon ridge fading into hazed desert,
here and there a sign of aquifers
and one possible watering-hole. If this were a
map
it would be the map of the last age of her life,

---

not a map of choices but a map of variations
on the one great choice. It would be the map by which
she could see the end of touristic choices,
of distances blued and purpled by romance,
by which she would recognize that poetry
isn't revolution but a way of knowing
why it must come. If this cheap, massproduced
wooden stand from the Brooklyn Union Gas Co.,
massproduced yet durable, being here now,
is what it is yet a dream-map
so obdurate, so plain,
she thinks, the material and the dream can join
and that is the poem and that is the late report.

Luis Rodríguez[*]
2006 Border Voices Poetry Fair

"Luis Rodriguez is the poet laureate of the barrio." — **Luis Torres,** radio journalist

BARE-BONES BIO: A former heroin addict and gang member, Luis Rodríguez has transformed himself into one of the nation's leading Chicano writers. He's won national awards for his poetry and children's books, while his memoir of gang life (*Always Running: La Vida Loca, Gang Days in L.A.*) was an international best seller. He insists that "it is time for the dispossessed to lead. You, the abandoned mother . . . You who are without a job or place called home. Study and be free." And he's backed his words with action, conducting workshops and readings in prisons, juvenile facilities, homeless shelters and migrant camps. "Rodríguez is a relentless truth-teller, an authentic visionary, a man of profound compassion" (*Los Angeles Times Book Review*).

---

[*] Photo by Donna DeCesare.

A FEW NOTES ABOUT THE POEM (AND A BIT MORE BIOGRAPHY): Luis Rodríguez is an extraordinarily engaging and lovable storyteller. Part of his charm comes from his ability to laugh at himself, and to help us see the humor in our own lives. All of us, for example, have battled cockroaches, all of us have gone to the garden shop to buy the "heavy artillery." Like Don Quixote, we frequently duel with giants that are giants only in our imaginations; and like Cervantes — the greatest of all Spanish writers and Rodríguez's poetic godfather — we know, in our saner moments, that we really AREN'T knights, sent to vanquish these mythical / miniscule enemies (at least, not all the time).

Mockery of shared foibles also appears in Rodríguez's poem "Fat," although here the humor has a sharper edge:

> We're all fat in America, even the anorexics,
> Fat with fat lies and fat fears and fat schemes. I've been fat for fifteen years — and exercise
> Pills, diets, doctors, stress, and Trader Joe's
> Food can't change that. This fat covers
> Sorrows, past indiscretions, slow death . . .
>
> No matter, we're all fat in America.
> Even thin models are full of themselves.

This discerning humor balances the other, more publicized and hugely controversial side of Rodríguez: his role as a crusader for social justice, carrying dark truths into places where they are sometimes VERY unwelcome. His memoir *Always Running* — with its graphic depictions of gang life — has been called one of the 100 most-censored books in the United States, and heated battles to remove his books from public-school libraries and reading lists have occurred in Illinois, Michigan, Texas, and California.

Despite the controversy, *Always Running* earned a Carl Sandburg Literary Award and was designated a *New York Times* Notable Book. Luis Rodríguez is also author of *Hearts and Hands: Creating Community in Violent Times* and a short story collection *The Republic of East LA: Stories.* His first novel, *Music of the Mill* (Rayo Books/HarperCollins), was published in May 2005. *My Nature is Hunger* (Curbstone Press, fall 2005) was his fourth poetry collection.

Luis Rodríguez was one of 50 leaders worldwide selected as "Unsung Heroes of Compassion," an award presented by the Dalai Lama in May 2001.

Rodríguez's determination to help the nation's youth grew out of his own experience with gangs, as well as the experience of his son Ramiro, sentenced to 28 years in prison for attempted murder. "The honest truth is I wasn't a good father," Rodríguez says. Now, he works to help kids "stop being instruments of their own death."

The Cockroaches I Married*

My cockroaches have been with me like forever:
Several generations of roach families
have graced my cupboards and book shelves
for around thirty years.
They are likely related to the critters
I encountered when I first married.
Although my wife and I eventually
broke up, these cockroaches continued to haunt
my socks drawer and toaster.
Over the years, regardless of where I lived,
I've carried these roaches in boxes,
magazines, clothes, and electrical appliances.
They nestled in the crumpled creases
and the darkest recesses.
(I trust it was them — the darn things do look
alike.)
Besides, every landlord I knew claimed
no roaches existed in their places
until I showed up!
Over time, I've tried everything to get rid
of the damn pests:
Bug sprays,
cucumber slices laid out in various corners,
roach motels,
and Chinese anti-roach chalk.
But somehow a few managed to survive
and stow away in my possessions
until I arrived at my next abode.

If I paid attention, I could have given
these creatures their own names:
Le Roché,
Cuca Rocha,
or *Lord Bugingham.*
They may end up as life-long partners;
they have outlasted most of my wives,
cars and jobs.
But over the years, I've accumulated
some horror stories.
Like when my kids were babies,
I'd turn on the lights and watch
cockroaches scurry across their small faces.
And I recall opening cereal boxes
from where the creatures scrutinized me
through bent antennas and beady eyes.
Or drinking coffee with roach pieces floating on
top.
Miserable spawn.
Disease carriers.
Blatta orientalis.
Despite this, we lived for a long time
in a kind of human-insect détente.
Whereas, I once took morbid pleasure
in crushing their hideous, brown-winged bodies,
I soon allowed them to meander by
without crashing down on them
with my fist.
One morning, though, the cold war
escalated to a fighting war:
My teenage son woke up the household
with blood yells down the hall.
As he held his head in a tortured expression,
he cried out about the pain.
I drove him to the hospital, where a doctor

— who looked like he had been through
much cockroach combat — took out
a tiny vacuum cleaner, stuck it gently
into my son's ear, and sucked up a particularly
gruesome mother.
That did it. I had reached my limits:
I brought in the heavy artillery.
An exterminator arrived with the latest
pest control technology,
including using enzymes that stopped
a roach's outer shell from growing:
They were crushed by their own bodies.
(What a way to go).
I know, in the end, they'll probably win.
But the fight, I tell you, the fight's the thing.
Nowadays, I may spot a lone roach warrior,
but I've carried out the equivalent
of chemical warfare and economic sanctions.
It's me or the roaches, man.
As far as I'm concerned,
this partnership is over. *Punto y zas.*

Gary Snyder
1995 Border Voices Poetry Fair

Gary Snyder — former Zen monk and lumberjack, counterculture hero and sometime-hermit (as well as a guy who's always been GREAT at a party) is — more than anyone else — the Mystery Man of modern poetry, the stranger at the gate, that fellow NOBODY can quite figure out . . .

We can date the start of the mystery almost to the minute: it was Oct. 7, 1955, and the place was a run-down art mart called Six Gallery in San Francisco. Six poets were reading, including a sweaty guy in a charcoal grey suit and white shirt named Allen Ginsberg, who was about to bust up the literary world and generate all sorts of hysteria about how terribly obscene his great new poem was: "I saw the best minds of my generation destroyed by madness . . . "

And there in the back of the room, wearing a then-unfashionable pair of blue jeans, was Poet #6, a quiet guy who was (according to a friend who was with him) "somehow certain of immortality, back then. In an impoverished Taoist unpublished poet sort of way. 'Save the invitation

254

(to the Six Gallery reading),' Gary confided, 'Some day it will be worth something.'"

And so it was, of course . . . and that Snyder knew this, somehow foresaw his own fame and Ginsberg's fame and all that was about to happen as a whole generation erupted into the great mad party that was the Sixties in America, is something that the young people who worshipped him believe even now, part of the Snyder mystique . . .

Part of this mystique is based on hyperbole, of course — memories gilded by time and bedecked with myth. But part of the mystique is based on something very real and puzzling and admirable in the history of this man and his groundbreaking poetry, something we can only sketch in the limited space we have here

Long before it was fashionable or even thought of, Gary Snyder began a spiritual journey that led him to the Far East via San Francisco, where he was one of the "Dharma Bums" and shared a cabin with novelist Jack Kerouac . . . still unknown, Snyder went to Japan, where he spent most of his time from 1956 to 1968, confronting visions of destruction and absolute nothingness in a Zen monastery and learning to live in the moment . . .

And then he came back to the United States, and by that time he was famous: there in his Zen monastery (and even before that, and certainly after) he had crafted poems like nothing anyone had seen before, poems as simple as a walk on a mountain trail, as profound as the sight of snow melting, your love turning from you in the icy air . . . and then he became an ecologist, practically founded the whole environmental movement . . . and . . . and . . .

Gary Snyder has published sixteen books of poetry and prose, including *The Gary Snyder Reader (1952-1998)* (Counterpoint Press, 1999); *Mountains and Rivers Without End* (1996); *No Nature: New and Selected Poems* (1993), which was a finalist for the National Book Award; *The Practice of the Wild* (1990); *Left Out in the Rain, New Poems 1947-1985*; *Axe Handles* (1983), for which he received an American Book Award; *Turtle Island* (1974), which won the Pulitzer Prize for poetry; *Regarding Wave* (1970); and *Myths & Texts* (1960). He has received an American Academy of Arts and Letters award, the Bollingen Prize, a Guggenheim Foundation fellowship, the Bess Hokin Prize and the Levinson Prize from *Poetry*, the Robert Kirsch Lifetime Achievement Award from the *Los Angeles Times*, and the Shelley Memorial Award. Snyder was elected a Chancellor of The Academy of American Poets in 2003. He is a professor of English at the University of California, Davis.

Instructions*

Fuel filler cap
>   — haven't I seen this before? The
>   sunlight under the eaves, mottled
>   shadow, on the knurled rim of
>   dull silver metal

Oil filler cap
>   bright yellow,
>   horns like a snail
>   — the oil's down there —
>   amber, clean, it
>   falls back to its pit

Oil drain plug
>   so short, from in to out. Best
>   let it drain when it is hot

Engine switch
>   Off, on. Off, on. Just
>   two places. Forever,

>   or, not even one.

EDITOR'S NOTE: The above version of Gary
Snyder's poem is EXACTLY as it appeared in
Mountains and Rivers Without End in 1996. Lit-

---

* Copyright © by Gary Snyder. When this poem was origi-
nally published, in the second Border Voices anthology in
1995, it was part of a work-in-progress that became *Moun-
tains and Rivers Without End*, which some critics have de-
scribed as Snyder's finest work. The book (Washington,
D.C.: Counterpoint) was published in 1996.

erary historians might be interested in comparing that final version of the poem with the draft that Snyder contributed to the 1995 Border Voices anthology. Here's that earlier version of the poem:

Instructions (early draft)

Fuel filler cap
> — haven't I seen this before? The
> sunlight under the eaves, mottled
> shadow, on the knurled rim of
> dull silver metal

oil filler cap
> bright yellow, horns
> like a snail — the oil is
> in there — amber, clean, it
> falls back to its pit

oil drain plug
> so short, from in to out. Best
> let it drain when it is hot

engine switch
> off, on, — off, on, — just
> two places. forever,

> or, not even one.

Gary Soto
1994 and 2002 Border Voices Poetry fairs

Gary Soto is "probably the best Chicano poet at work nowadays . . . (he seems) almost incapable of writing bad poems."
— **James White**

BARE-BONES BIO: Gary Soto recalls that when he was a Mexican-American boy growing up in Fresno, "we didn't have many books around . . . and no one really encouraged us to read. In fact, I never thought about being a writer when I was a kid." How things have changed. A list of Soto's books covers half a page of dense copy, and his well-  earned literary awards cover another half-page. He is a poet and short-story writer, essayist and film producer, and has taught at UC Berkeley, UC Riverside, and (during a lightning visit to San Diego in 2002) at Border Voices workshops at Pershing Middle School, where he wowed and inspired students and teachers alike with his engaging humor. His books have become a sta-

259

ple in classrooms at major universities as well as elementary, middle and high schools.

TIPS FOR YOUNG WRITERS: Gary Soto's poems have many of the same qualities as his fiction: they are engaging, humorous, perceptive, and detailed in their re-creation of the life of Hispanics in the United States. Because Soto's prose works are of greater length than his poems, and because the poems share the relatively uncompressed and colloquial qualities of the fiction, his short stories tend to generate more power. Nevertheless, Soto is one of the foremost Hispanic poets in 21st Century America.

His life is also a lesson in overcoming discouragement. As a young man, he enrolled for a class with Philip Levine, one of the great teachers of verse and a Pulitzer Prize winner. "I brought him a poem I wrote, something about a giant cockroach," Soto recalled during his 2002 visit to San Diego's Pershing Middle School. "He read it, and he started laughing. He kept laughing all the way through." It was not good laughter. "I went home and wrote another poem about a giant cockroach, only this time it was better," Soto said. He has never looked back, and his sweetly sad and humorous short stories about life in the barrio — such as the award-winning *Petty Crimes* — have made him a favorite with readers of all races. (Soto's appeal to young people was dramatically illustrated at the 2002 Border Voices Poetry Fair, where he was mobbed by youngsters who'd read his children's books. The besieged Soto grinned sheepishly at a sympathetic onlooker: "My fans," he said. "Ain't it somethin'?")

260

A GARY-SOTO-READING-LIST, & OTHER INFO: Gary Soto is the author of numerous books of poetry, including *New and Selected Poems* (Chronicle Books, 1995), which was a National Book Award finalist; *Canto Familiar/Familiar Song* (1994); *Neighborhood Odes* (1992); *Home Course in Religion* (1991); *Who Will Know Us?* (1990); *Black Hair* (1985); *Where Sparrows Work Hard* (1981); *The Tale of Sunlight* (1978); and *The Elements of San Joaquin* (1977). Soto has also written two novels, *Poetry Lover* (University of New Mexico Press, 2001) and *Nickel and Dime* (2000); the memoir *Living Up the Street* (1985), for which he received an American Book Award; numerous young adult and children's books; and edited three anthologies: *Pieces of Heart* (1993), *California Childhood* (1988), and *Entrance: Four Latino Poets* (1976). He is one of the youngest poets to appear in *The Norton Anthology of Modern Poetry*, and he even wrote a libretto for an opera entitled *Nerd-landia*. His honors include the Andrew Carnegie Medal, the United States Award of the International Poetry Forum, *The Nation* / "Discovery" Prize, and the Bess Hokin Prize and the Levinson Award from *Poetry*. He has also received fellowships from the California Arts Council, the Guggenheim Foundation, and the National Endowment for the Arts.

Field Poem[*]

When the foreman whistled
My brother and I shouldered our hoes,
We returned to the bus speaking
In broken English, in broken Spanish
The restaurant food,
The tickets to a dance
We wouldn't buy with our day's pay.

From the smashed bus window,
I saw the leaves of cotton plants
Like small hands waving good-bye.

Berkeley Dogs[†]

The dogs look human in their Volvos,
Or so I discover as I walk through the
      parking lot of Longs Drugs,
Swinging my small purchase of antacids
      and vanilla ice cream.
All the dogs sit in their rightful place,
      the windows cracked.
Their mugs convey the look of, "No,
      I'm not what you think."
I call, "Hey, boy," to one pup who
      turns its head away, disgusted.
I call, "Hey, lassie," to a Golden Retriever.
      To make her point,

She places her paws onto the steering wheel.
These dogs don't bark. Their eyes form
      words that say, "Go away."
I don't. When I look into the window
      of one car,
The dog busies itself checking the odometer
      for the next oil change.
How did this happen, this evolution
      in less than thirty years?
The pooches of my own childhood
      street fetched and frolicked,
Fought themselves into bloody rags.
      They copulated in fury,
As we kids hollered, amazed by the
      pushpush action in the middle
Of the street. These Berkeley dogs
      practice their Zen
With the feng shui of water bowls set half-in,
      half-out of shadows.
These dogs know how to roll with Aikido.
They have lawyers, too, when divorce occurs
And resolution counselors when a fuss rises up
      between different breeds.
They know their rights.

The moon has no influence on these canines.
And moon now rides high over the parking lot
      of Longs Drugs.
By this light I see a dog in every parked car
      reading the Wall Street Journal.
I'm still where I always was, a male dog
      with Playboys in the bottom drawer.
They have shifted from the back seat,
      to the passenger's seat,
To finally the driver's seat. When one set

Of owners returns from the store, they
      get into the back.
The dog gazes in the rearview mirror to see
      if its companions
Are buckled in, for they share in wills and deeds.
The Volvo starts with a shiver, leaves cautiously.
The companions smile at each other. They take
up   leashes
In their mouths, sniffing for the future.

Mark Strand[*]

2000 Border Voices Poetry Fair

Mark Strand is the former Poet Laureate of the United States, a Pulitzer Prize winner — and apparently an enigma even to his admirers, who heap him with awards while disagreeing PROFOUNDLY about what he has to say.

For those new to Strand's work, we can illustrate the problem by quoting one of his most popular and anthologized poems, "Eating Poetry":

Ink runs from the corners of my mouth.
There is no happiness like mine
I have been eating poetry . . .

The poems are gone.
The light is dim.
The dogs are on the basement stairs and coming up . . .

The poor librarian begins to stamp her feet and weep.
She does not understand.
When I get on my knees and lick her hand,
she screams.

I am a new man,

---

[*] Photo by Lilo Raymond.

I snarl at her and bark.
I romp with joy in the bookish dark.

It is poems like these that caused the literary historian David Perkins, a brilliant and usually flawless analyst of contemporary poetry, to describe Strand as a "Surrealist." But as *The Norton Anthology of Modern Poetry* has pointed out, Strand's poems are not really Surrealist. There are none of the terrible disjunctions and disruptions of language found in the Surrealists, no absurd cartoon-like configurations of imagery (e.g., "hungry fanged roses mate in the mailed garden.") "Eating Poetry" is no exception to this: despite its superficially bizarre story-line, the poem is not absurdist, and it is not a cartoon; instead, it offers a compelling and precise description of spiritual-aesthetic transfiguration.

In it, Strand joyfully describes what it feels like to give yourself up to a great poet, to fill your ear and imbue your spirit with the rhythms and the world view of (say) a Yeats or a Rilke. The result is transformation: "I romp with joy in the bookish dark . . . "

Strand has also sought this sense of transformation through the act of writing his OWN poems, and has been honest enough to hint that he has not always been successful. For example, in one early and desperate poem a character is shown sleeping in a soundless room where "nothing curled in the air / but the sound of nothing, / the hymn of nothing . . . "

The critic David Kirby has described Strand as seeking "self-effacement" through his poetry; it is probably more accurate to describe him as a man in search of a skin that fits in these often-terrible times. He finds it, sometimes, in the art of poetry; and his joyous and occasionally terrifying discoveries are a gift to all of us.

A PERSONAL NOTE FROM THE EDITOR: The first time I read "Eating Poetry" I felt like I was reading the freshest and most exciting stuff to hit the page since T.S. Eliot was a young man wearing green makeup (really) at his secret flat on Charing Cross Road . . . Strand's poetry reminded me of the pebbles in the Zbigniew Herbert poem: "Pebbles cannot be tamed / to the end they will look at us / with a calm and very clear eye." When I held Strand's poems in my mental grip, they seemed to shiver, they opened their eyes, they LOOKED at me . . .
And they still do.

Lake*

To drowse away the summer on a lake
*
To feel the limitations of the lake
*
To count the lake's two colors
*
To feel that something is wrong with the lake
*
I really like the lake, said the woman next door
*

---

* © 1999 by Mark Strand. The poem entered the world (received its first publication anywhere) in the seventh annual Border Voices anthology in 2000.

You push a lake out of the way, but it comes
right   back

*

A lake could mean the end of chaos

*

A lake swallows itself every night

*

I like this lake, too, I said to the woman next
door

*

There once was a lake with only one wave

*

Fifty young men were staring into the lake

*

If you speak to the lake, you must ask yourself
why

*

To test the true material of the lake

*

To dip the oars of sleep into the surface of the
lake

*

To feel the lake give birth to words for itself

*

A lake could fall into the wrong hands

*

Even an artificial lake needs real water

*

Oh the lake is beautiful, and meaningless, and I
love it

*

What lake is that you're talking about

*

No lake at all — I'm bad at remembering lakes

*

Is it the way a lake looks or how it feels that
matters

*

In that respect a lake is like a chair

*

The lake was full of stars, the moon, the tops of
trees

*

Someone was playing a trombone across the
lake

*

On this side of the lake a silence was building
up

Ken Waldman[*]
2004 and 2006 Border Voices Poetry fairs

BARE-BONES BIO: Alaska's fiddlin' poet has been praised as "a music-man in more ways than one," crafting poems that are "rich with lively imagery and characters" (Naomi Shihab Nye). An Alaska resident for more than 20 years, Waldman now tours the United States full time, fiddle case in hand. He has published more than 400 poems and stories in national magazines, and his Appalachian-style music and engaging verse have been showcased at some of the country's leading clubs, bookstores, universities and art festivals. His most recent books are *And Shadow Remained* and *The Secret Visitor's Guide*, while his music can be found on CDs with engaging titles such as "Fiddling Poets on Parade" (a children's CD) and "All Originals, All Traditionals."

A FEW NOTES ABOUT THE POEMS (AND A BIT MORE BIOGRAPHY): As these words are being typed, one of Ken Waldman's CDs is playing in the background. It's "Fiddling Poets on Pa-

---

[*] Photo by Kate Wool

rade," subtitled "Alaskan Fiddling Poet Music for kids of all ages," and it's full of the bounce and lilt of fiddle music interspersed — at the moment — with Ken Waldman's distinctive voice imitating dog barks and whines (it's a VERY sad dog). And now here's another tune, and Waldman's voice singing about "old Joe Clark."

Waldman is quite right. As he said in an interview, he can't sing. But it hardly matters. As Jean Greenwood of the University of Wisconsin wrote, Waldman's inability to sing "is just one aspect of a wondrous, prodigious, and indescribably unique talent that can only be defined as, well, 'The Ken Waldman poetry/fiddling/non-singing thing' . . . Otherwise sensible people have been known to hurry out the next day and purchase a fiddle and fiddle lessons after a Waldman concert . . . He's that kind of a guy . . . Like Oshkosh B'Gosh overalls, he is, indeed, the genuine article."

Waldman has created his own approach to art, carrying it around the country in a battered minivan, writing endless letters to just about anyone who might be interested in his work, and he has loads of poems published in magazines, and — count 'em — SEVEN books looking for publishers, including collections of poems, a novel set in Alaska, and two memoirs.

As he said in a recent letter, "My joke these past few years was I'd either get established or go bankrupt. Now, it seems, having just turned 50, I'm simultaneously approaching both."

All this is by way of introduction to the accompanying two poems, in each of which Waldman does something rare and precious in an age of cynicism: he embraces another human being with unqualified affection and hopefulness.

In "A Happier Doctor," Waldman celebrates a woman who, having made choices that defined her life, learns to love the results. And in "Treble Choir Was Her World," the poet sings of a young girl who — like Waldman himself — shone with light and gave birth to a voice, despite all obstacles.

As he says, he speaks to children of all ages. Listen to him.

AND A QUICK P.S.: The above "bare-bones bio" and other notes were written early in 2006, and were an accurate description of Waldman's work up to that time. But this is a man who churns out poetry, novels, music, etc., faster than snowflakes fall in an Alaskan blizzard, and by the time this update was being prepared in October 2006, Waldman had turned to a new field — political satire — with his book *As the World Burns: The Sonnets of George W. Bush.* Those desiring to keep up with this peripatetic poet should visit his Web site, kenwaldman.com.

Treble Choir Was Her World*

Inside her throat, light
shined so bright, it grew
into a bird. She named that bird
Voice. It sang and sang.
Dance teachers tried to quash it
with point shoes. Art teachers
tried to tar its white feathers
with paints. Schoolteachers
tried to talk it to death.
Voice only knew to fly
out of her mouth
and soar for the flock.

A Happier Doctor†

  — for Julia

Yet another practice to begin. Magic
maybe, doctor as juggler, a dozen
roles cascading: mother and daughter; wife,
midwife, analyst; linguist
and listener; dancer, driver, chef;

---

* Copyright © 2006 by Ken Waldman. From *Conditions and Cures*, Steel Toe Books, Bowling Green KY, 2006. (The poem was also published in the 13th annual Border Voices anthology, in March 2006. It is reprinted here by permission of the author).
† Copyright © 2004 by Ken Waldman. When it first appeared in the 11th annual Border Voices anthology, in 2004, this poem was previously unpublished. In 2006, it was included in Waldman's *Conditions and Cures* (Steel Toe Books, Bowling Green KY). It is reprinted here with the permission of the author.

healer and boss. Ah, the losses
you can now accept, the lives unlived:
local activist, global wanderer, Olympic
gymnast, grant-mad research guru, hermit
glassblower, book critic for *The Times*.
Some late afternoon in that blessed space
between patients, you'll have to place
the stethoscope to your own heart,
replay that path from happy to happier,
make the first move toward happiest.

Sherley Anne Williams
1994 Border Voices Poetry Fair

" . . . it is precisely because I am a single mother of an only son that I try hard to (write poetry and stories based on my life). Women must leave a record for their men; otherwise how will they know us?"
— Sherley Anne Williams (1944-1999)

It's just so damned SAD . . . there is such a deep pit of MISERY in the phrase "brilliant but neglected author," especially when they say it about someone like Sherley Anne Williams — she of the

bright and beautiful mind, the woman who won an Emmy for her stunning TV recitation of poems from the book *SomeOne Sweet Angel Chile.* Her wonderful first novel, *Dessa Rose,* was named a *New York Times* Notable Book when it came out in 1986, she was raved about as the next Langston Hughes, a writer of unlimited potential . . .

And now, seven years after her death, you can buy *Dessa Rose* for $.01 at amazon.com. (That is NOT a typo! The book is on sale for ONE CENT). And some of her other books are there

275

too, also at miserably low prices. And the sales rankings! I mean, my gawd, Ernest Hemingway's *A Moveable Feast*, published way back in 1964, after the man was already DEAD, is listed as one of the top sellers on amazon.com, ranked 37,836. Dessa Rose is down there at 874,095 — meaning more than 800,000 books are more popular than her one-time best seller. And some of her other books fare even worse — *Girls Together* ranks at 1,498,999, can be bought for $1.25, and received ZERO customer reviews (compared to 125 reviews for the Hemingway book).

Those who love Williams and her work know that tastes change, audiences and critics are fickle — after all, Shakespeare himself went out of fashion in the 17th and 18th centuries, with critics accusing him of corrupting the language, artistic ineptitude etc. etc.

But Williams isn't being criticized: in some way she has fallen off the map of literary America . . . except for those who love her. And those who love her are people of very good taste indeed. Philip Levine, he of the Pulitzer Prize and the towering talent, was one of her teachers, and he was devastated by her death: "She was one of the two most inspiring students I've had in forty years of teaching . . . you're not supposed to outlive your students." In an essay in the *Lincoln Centre Review* in Spring 2005, Levine said that Williams taught him how to be a better writer and . . . even more importantly . . . a better MAN.

With so much respect flowing in Williams' direction from people who COUNT, it's hard to believe that a revival will never occur. What she had to say still resonates somewhere, deep down, a thrumming echo that people who love poetry feel and treasure. It will resonate on a larger scale, someday ...

Oh well. Read the accompanying poem, Sherley Anne Williams' tribute to her son. Try to picture Williams, uncharacteristically shy that day, reading it at the first Border Voice fair back in 1994. Think of the reasons she wrote . . . to free the voice of her race, to <u>leave</u> something for her son . . . it reminds me somehow of Auden's great elegy for Yeats, something about what it is that survives the writer after his or her death . . . here, let me look it up for you . . .

for poetry makes nothing happen: it . . .
                        . . . flows on south
From ranches of isolation and the busy griefs,
Raw towns that we believe and die in; it survives,
A way of happening, a mouth.
          — W.H. Auden
               from "In Memory of W.B. Yeats"

I see my life . . .*

I

I see my life by my son's
eyes   know his mind is in some
part my own   that he carries
me as he moves through the world.
I am some percent of the
sum of my mother and my
father   of the grandparents
the old ones from whom I get
the shape of my hands   my head
maybe my walk and the eyes
that stare from this face. I don't
know all that comes through them to
me and him who are now their
factors in the world. Yet I
am me; he is he.

II

We're named
in the sight of the people
in our family houses
in each of our own hearts. I
didn't learn how to call myself
until I was twenty-four.
I cling to the secret child-
hood names only a very

---

* "I see my life . . . " by Sherley Anne Williams. From *The Peacock Poems*, published by Wesleyan University Press. Copyright © 1975 by Sherley Williams. Reprinted by permission. (This poem was also printed in the first Border Voices anthology, in 1994, with the permission of the author).

278

few can know.
                    I gave my son
four names; he added two more.
In the privacy of his
own room he calls himself by
others I may never know.

III

My son springs up from the bottom
of the pool   head back   eyes closed
water sheeting his body
with light and caught like stars in
the dark burrs of his hair. It's
not the sun whose shine dances
on the waves. That is his face.
And although I see the name
he has named himself I would
never tell it even if
my mind   my mouth   could say it.

Acknowledgements

Border Voices — and, by extension, this book — is the result of a collaboration between dozens of poets, teachers and organizations who are determined to bring opportunities for literary creativity to our children. Among those who have supported Border Voices with both donations and encouragement over the years are the Helen K. and James S. Copley Foundation; the Dempster-Larsen Fund of The Parker Foundation; the San Diego Commission for Arts and Culture; the John R. and Jane F. Adams Endowment; the California Arts Council; the Szekely Family Foundation; the Fieldstone Foundation; Audrey Geisel and the Dr. Seuss Foundation; the National Endowment for the Art, and Poets & Writers, Inc.

Gratitude is also owed members of the Border Voices board: Janet Delaney, director of Community Relations, San Diego Unified; Danah Fayman, philanthropist and creator of the San Diego Arts Foundation and Partners for Livable Places; Joy Hanna, former board member of Friends of the San Diego Public Library; Carleen Hemric, who is also a board member for three other organizations: Greater San Diego County Council of Teachers of English, the California Association of Teachers of English (CATE), and the umbrella Friends of the San Diego Public Library; Blue Robbins, SDSU cultural arts manager; Eugene Stein, director of sponsored research development, SDSU Research Foundation; Stephen L. Weber, president, San Diego State University; John Weil, financial planner and investment manager, and a member of several boards of directors in San Diego; Catherine Yi-yu Cho Woo, SDSU professor emeritus who served on the National Council for the Arts for both the first President Bush and for William Jefferson Clinton; Elizabeth Y. Yamada, a former partner at Wimmer, Yamada and Caughey landscape architecture firm and a former member of the San Diego Commission for Arts and Culture.

Thanks also to Frea Sladek, former board member and former chief executive officer of the SDSU Research Foundation: her creativity and steady support will be missed. And a big "thank you" as well to Joan Webb, secretary to the board, for her efficient and cheerful support.

We're also grateful to the coterie of volunteer administrators who keep everything running smoothly through hard work leavened with humor, including Chris Baron, who has served 10 years as fair manager at the annual Border Voices poetry festival; Veronica Cunningham; and Chris Dickerson and Celia Sigmon, who edit the annual anthology with the help of Seretta Martin. Seretta has also provided inestimable aid to the project director (an admitted and unapologetic technophobe) by overseeing the Web site ...

And a VERY special thanks to *The San Diego Union-Tribune* for agreeing to co-sponsor the project, and to publish student poems and artwork in the newspaper at the time of the annual fair. Members of the *Union-Tribune* staff have expended many hours on the project, and the following list is not exhaustive: Vincent DePalma, the ever-helpful and conscientious community relations representative; Leslie L.J. Reilly, the graphic artist who designs the annual anthology, the fair poster, and other odds and ends, delighting everyone with her cheerful brilliance; Drew Schlosberg, community and public relations manager; Margo Raynes, who helps coordinate *Union-Tribune* efforts on behalf of Border Voices. Finally, we would like to express our deep appreciation to Karin Winner, editor of the *Union-Tribune*, for her continuing support over the years.

We also offer our deep appreciation to the 13 Border Voices poets who are currently going into San Diego County classrooms to teach the art of verse: James D. Babwe, Francisco Bustos, Brandon Cesmat, Veronica Cunningham, Gloria Foster, Jackleen Holton, Georgette James, Paula Jones, Roxanne Young Kilbourne, Seretta Martin, Jill Moses, Johnnierenee Nia Nelson, and Celia Sigmon.

The work of former poet-teachers is also deeply appreciated: Jim Allen, Carmen Aravena, Claudia Axel, Julia Doughty, Steven Garber, Jana Gardner, Tamara Johnson, Jim Milner, Joe Milosch, minerva (Gail Hawkins), Andres Monreal, Nicholas Moramarco, Reggie Morin, Kathleen Shumate, Gabriela Anaya Valdepeña, Mary Williams, Sabrina Youmans, and Sandra Zane.

Following is a list of others who have contributed money or other support (in-kind, moral or logistical) to the Border Voices Poetry Project:

The Administrators Association of San Diego City Schools; the Associated Students of San Diego State University; the Association of San Diego Educators of the Gifted; Barnes & Noble/Bookstar; Borders Books & Music; California Poets in the Schools; the San Diego Chargers; the College of Arts and Letters, SDSU; the San Diego County Office of Education, with special thanks to Dr. Rudy M. Castruita, superintendent, and Richard A. Harrison; the Greater San Diego Council of Teachers of English; the San Diego Padres; and Anne Stoup and Ken Packer, Aztec Shops.

Thanks, too, to the San Diego Unified School District, with special thanks to the Office of School Site Support, Instruction and Curriculum. We are grateful for the help of dozens of other administrators and teachers in the district, and will pick one to represent them all: Sarah Sullivan, principal of Pershing Middle School, who helped the Border Voices Poetry Project organize and document one of its most ambitious programs — a full year of poetry workshops at the school, involving every student; with followup monitoring of standardized testing through 2004. Additional and sincere appreciation goes to the National School District and its staff, teachers and administrators for their many years of active involvement in the project.

Finally, the volunteers of Border Voices wish to express their appreciation to William H. Roetzheim, founder and chief executive officer of Level 4 Press, Inc., for his love and support of poetry, as well as his vision in publishing this book.

Index by Poet/Illustrator

Index by Title

Index by Poet Teacher

Index by Teacher

Index by School